sharin' the craic *

Irish Tales from a Grateful American

Book 2

By J.J. McCormack

SHARIN' THE FUN*

Dedication

To the warmth and humor of the Irish.

Acknowledgements

I would like to thank my husband Brian for holding down the fort at home while I embarked on my adventure, and for his wonderful support throughout. My friends and family for reading the journals in their raw form and for their love and encouragement. A few of them I will name, but there will be many who, while not named here for the sake of brevity, know who they are.

Katherine Vanzwoll a fellow writer and friend. Kimberly Kauffman for being a faithful and enthusiastic reader. Dawn Bassett for a lifetime of being my partner in crime and for braving Conor Pass, all for the sake of a good story. Nate and Karen Kauffman for encouraging me to publish my Ireland journals. Jeremy Lounds for his expertise in bringing this book to publication and for his constant good nature and patience with my technological ignorance.

At last, to the people I met on my travels in beautiful Connemara.

Author's Note

This collection of short stories are true accounts of some of my magical experiences in Irish fishing villages and are as close to verbatim as my memory and notes could reproduce. Names of people and specific locations have been changed or omitted to protect the privacy of the people characterized within.

To capture the lyrical charm of the country and its people, I have used phonetic spelling to recreate the Irish brogue in the dialogue. I found that, without the nuances and rhythms of speech, the stories lost some of their magic. I followed this same line of thinking when writing about my encounter with Shanika of the Detroit Airport Personnel. My decision to embrace the dialects in prose is intended with respect and to honor the spirit of the speaker.

A note about the pubs: Pubs are the primary places you will find people, particularly in January. Following the story means following the people, and pubs are the social hub of the Irish culture.

At last, you may note the significant degree to which the F-Word is used throughout the dialogue in these stories. This is not due to my particular penchant for such colorful language, but is, instead, a common representation of the manner of speaking favored in the wild Connemara. By the time I headed back home to Michigan, the word no longer even registered as swearing.

Table of Contents

Prologue:

Embarking on
Irish Fishing Village Number Two

When my first solitary trip to Ireland came to an end, I went back to my life in the States, but Ireland wasn't far from my mind. I couldn't wait to return to this enchanted island in the middle of the Atlantic, anxious to meet more interesting people.

A wonderful thing about the first village I'd visited was that, by the time I left, I had made many friends, people with whom I have kept in touch via text and email during the year in between. The down side was that, for this village and its people, I would never again have the experience of being a stranger in a strange land. In addition, returning to the same village would not allow me to compare cultural variations from one village to the next.

For these reasons, as January rolled around again, I prepared for another trip, choosing to spend the bulk of my time in a different fishing village farther up the west coast.

Visiting my Irish friends in the first village would mean braving the public bus system, but with one month abroad under my belt, I decided I was up for the challenge.

Thanks so much for joining me in this, my second Irish adventure!

CHAPTER 1

Shanika the Vegetarian Refuses to be a Cannibal:

Education from a Student of Humanity

§ hanika is a long-suffering member of Detroit Airport Personnel. I met her when the Kiosk I was using refused to cooperate with any of my numerous attempts to obtain my boarding pass.

Shanika, otherwise known as my angel, has skin the color of dark chocolate. Her acrylic fingernails are bathed in tangerine glitter polish, the curved talon tips adorned with purple polka dots. Her halo of hair is the color of melted butterscotch.

Floating down from the heavens, or Break Room B-1, Shanika landed behind me, her voice a welcome foghorn in a mist shrouded sea. "You ain't never gon' check in that way. Get out the way; let me do dat fo' you."

Gratefully, I stepped aside. Taking my passport from my trembling fingers, she swept it deftly over the scanner, clicked some keys with those amazing purple polka dotted tips and, like magic, I was in.

"There you go, Darlin'," my angel said, pushing my passport back into my hand. "Now, you best check that bag fo' it falls over and crushes you to death."

I babbled my thanks and Shanika turned me in the direction of the bag checking counter.

"See, look there, you next in line."

It was just after 6:00 a.m. Noticing that my plane wasn't scheduled to board until 9:15, Shanika said, "You wasn't takin' no chances, was you, when you got here this mornin'?"

Recovering a few of my wayward social skills, I grinned at her and said, "I allowed myself an hour and a half for check-in."

Shanika grinned back, her broad face splitting into a wide, toothy smile. "Honey," she said. "You coulda' got here at midnight and you still wouldn't a had enough time to check in, not the way you was doin' it."

"The way I see it," I said, "My timing was damn near perfect."

Her grin grew even broader. "You all right. I like you."

Then, knitting her brow, she stared at me for a beat, then said, "I'm gon' stick with you a while, just until we get that monster bag of yours up on that scale. I don't know how the hell you got that thing in here, but I'd hate to see it kill you now when you so close to the finish line."

Though the airport was far from busy, the people ahead of me had run into a snag with their 6:00 a.m. flight to Ft. Lauderdale.

The woman assisting this couple, another of the airport angels, had kind eyes and patience beyond my powers of description.

While they, whom I'll refer to as Billy-Bob and Della-Ray, hollered variations of the phrase: "I can't fuckin' believe this," at the top of their lungs, their angel attempted to explain that no matter how fast they made it through security, they would never be able to catch a plane that had already taken off.

"Uh-huh," Shanika muttered as she stood next to me behind the white line. "That right there is why I became a vegetarian."

"Oh?" I said, not quite grasping the connection.

"Oh, don't worry, you not one of them. You smart enough; you just scared and not, you know, worldly. I can tell the difference. All I have to do is look at you to tell the difference.

"But them?" she said, nodding in the direction of tattooed, red-faced Billy-Bob and gum-popping, stringy-haired Della-Ray. "They ain't nothin' more than dumb animals. I deal with them every day in this job."

She paused to swivel her head from side to side, slow and deliberate, as if to note the shame and disgrace of the scene unfolding before us.

In that moment, I decided to risk lowering her estimation of my natural intelligence by asking the obvious question burning in the back of my throat. "I'm a huge animal lover so I think it's great that you're a vegetarian," I said. "But I don't quite understand what that has to do with...them." I gestured with my head toward Mr. and Mrs. Billy-Bob.

A slow smile spread across her features. "Ever since I was a little girl, I hear everybody in my family say it's okay to eat meat because they wasn't no more than dumb animals and God put them on the earth to feed us humans. It never did set right with me, but I guessed they probably knew what they was talkin' about.

"Then I took this job at the airport, and all I see, day in and day out, are these humans like them over there. Dumb as rocks, every one of 'em.

"Every four-legged animal I ever met is smarter than 98% of the people walkin' through these doors every day."

My angel Shanika paused for effect, then drove her point home. "And I says to myself, 'Shanika, if it's God's plan that you eat dumb animals, then God must want you to become a cannibal.'

"Well, I decided that didn't sound like the kinda plan God would come up with. The logic just didn't hold up no more.

"And that's why I became a vegetarian. Besides, lazy-ass people like that be way too chewy."

CHAPTER 2

Traveling Companions Brought Together by Fate

3 Stories

"Moira, terrified o' flyin', she is."

I was in the window seat on the flight from Boston to Ireland. Seated next to me was an Irish couple who'd just spent the holidays with their daughter. Donal was seated in the middle, while his wife had the aisle seat. Donal was friendly and talkative, Moira, silent and anxious, wringing her bejeweled, arthritic hands in her lap.

Leaning toward me, Donal whispered in my ear, "Terrified o' flyin', she is. Hasna' uttered a word since we

entered the airport. Under usual circumstances, I canno'
get her to shut up!"

No more than 15 minutes into the flight we hit
turbulence, and not just a little.

Moira peeped and clutched her red handbag with one
hand, holding fast to Donal with the other. "This is it," she
said in a shaky contralto. "We've dun it now, we have.
We'll be tumblin' out o' the sky at any moment."

The plane tipped and bobbed and the fasten seatbelt sign
blinked on. The pilot's voice came on over the intercom.
"As ye can tell by the feel o' things, we've hit a wee bit o'
bumpy air." The pilot of the Aer Lingus flight was also
Irish. "I suggest ye stay in yer seats. Dunna' be goin' to the
toilet 'til it's passed, er ye'll be regrettin' yer decision, sure
'nuff."

"That's it," Moira said again, her bright red fingernails
digging into both purse and husband, respectively. "We're
dead as doornails, we are. Colleen will na'er forgive
herself fer leavin' home. Serves her right fer marryin' a
damned American and movin' so feckin' far away. Didna'
I tell ye now, it would come to no good?"

"Aw an' Moira, dunna' be sayin' such things. We've a guest to our country ye'll be scarin' half to death," Donal said, motioning to me.

"Well, then she'll be halfway there when we fall out o' the sky."

Donal turned a pair of apologetic blue eyes in my direction, then turned back to his wife. Moira had begun to keen loudly, and sway back and forth with the movement of the plane.

"Moira, Sweetheart, please," Donal begged. "Ye'll be frightenin' the other passengers with all that buggerin' noise. Come now, be a good woman an' cuddle up next to me."

"I won't," she said sharply, interrupting her high-pitched moaning. "It's yer fault we're goin' to die here like a couple o' crows shot out o' the sky."

"I thought ye just said it was Colleen's fault."

"It's hers too. There's plenty o' blame to go 'round." And with that, she resumed her keening.

About Donal and Moira I had learned a lot, but Donal, having asked not a single question since taking our seats, knew nothing of me. Just as I was debating whether to let them know that I had some experience helping people who suffered from panic and anxiety, Moira began to hyperventilate.

Her breathing grew shallow and she began to wheeze, no longer able to muster enough air to support the godawful caterwauling of a moment before. But it wouldn't be long before she either passed out or lost her dinner, neither of which I relished, so quietly I offered my services to Donal. His look of relief and gratitude equaled that of a man lost at sea suddenly caught in the Coast Guard's spotlight.

Turning to his wife, he said, "Moira, we're in luck. The woman beside me here is a counselor. She'll be able to help ye out."

Moira raised brown, incredulous eyes to her husband's face and, between shuddering gasps of air, managed to say, "Does she have a parachute on her, then?"

I must admit, I enjoyed Moira's capacity to maintain her sardonic wit in a crisis.

"Come on now," Donal said, ignoring her sarcasm. "Switch seats wit' me." He stood, shifted and, lifting his wife bodily from her seat, plunked her down between us.

Offering her my hand, she grabbed on. I hadn't felt a grip like that since I'd accompanied a friend into the delivery room.

In low tones, I said, "Everything's going to be all right. All we have to do is breathe our way through this and things will even out again."

"How do ye know?" The words eeked out through red lips that stood out from a face white as paper. Her pleading eyes sought mine.

"I've flown a fair amount," I lied. "And there's often this level of turbulence. And the captain sounded very relaxed and casual."

"Means nuthin'," she wheezed. "He's probably drunk."

Okay, so appealing to her rational side wasn't likely to get us anywhere. I switched tactics. "I want you to breathe as I do. You have to watch and listen to me closely. Are you ready?"

She nodded. Instructions seemed to help.

I said, "I'm going to take a deep breath in through my nose. When I do, I'll squeeze your hand. You take it in with me and when I loosen my grip, that's your signal to let your breath out long and slow through your mouth. Got it?"

Again, she nodded, never taking her eyes from mine. Donal, now in the aisle seat, had lost interest and was complaining to the man across the way about how the flight attendants "refused to serve bevies just because o' a little problem wit' the air currents."

Three deep breaths later, Moira's breathing was back to normal and her grip on my hand no longer a killer crunch.

The turbulence had smoothed out, and she offered me a weak smile. "Yer a good wee lass, an' ye are," she said, back in full voice. "An' ye truly dunna' believe we're goin' to be crashin' anytime soon?"

I shook my head and smiled back at her. "I don't think so, no."

Her eyes searched mine for the truth behind the statement. Satisfied with what she saw, she gave an embarrassed little laugh and squeezed my hand with more affection than terror this time. "I suppose ye think I'm a daft old woman."

"Not at all," I said. "Lots of people are a little nervous when they fly. And everybody's afraid of something."

"A woman travelin' alone as ye are, I'll bet yer no' afraid o' nuthin'."

"Do you want to know the truth?" I asked and realized I was already beginning to turn my phrases in the way of the Irish.

Moira, nodding eagerly.

"I'm afraid of lots of things. That's the main motivation for traveling on my own. I want to conquer my fears."

She looked surprised. "Well, what do ye know?" Shaking her head, she cast her eyes down at our hands still clasped together. "I've always run from mine."

"Is fear of flying one of them?"

She grinned broadly, color flushing her cheeks, and her face, in that instant, turned pretty and young. "What tipped ye off?"

I laughed and gave her fingers another squeeze. "Doesn't look like you ran from this one."

Tears filled her eyes. Leaning close, she gave me an unexpected kiss on the cheek. When I went to the bathroom later in the flight, there was a perfect pair of red lips tattooed on the side of my face.

Waiting for the Bus from Shannon

The bus from Shannon International Airport to Galway was scheduled to arrive at 7:10 a.m. I learned this from a goth looking young man wearing an army surplus jacket in faded green who asked me for a fag as we stood together under the bus stop sign.

"Sorry, I don't smoke," I said, shivering in the unexpectedly chilly Shannon morning, my breath coming out in tiny puffs of frosty air. "I need to get to Galway. Am I at the right stop?"

Johnny nodded absently, having turned back to scan the airport entrance for fellow smokers from whom he might bum a cig. "That's right," he said. "Headed there meself to meet up wif' a girl I met in a chat room online. Irish, she is, wif' gobs o' gorgeous red hair if her pic ain't lyin'.

"Name's Johnny from Liverpool and you're not." He grinned at me, displaying a desperate need for dental work.

I smiled back, gave him my name and said, "I'm from the United States."

"Ah," said Johnny from Liverpool. "I know somfin' 'bout America. I'm a bit familiar like. What part you from?"

"The Midwest, Michigan."

"Hold on," he said. "I fink I spotted a bloke wif' a smoke. Be right back, then." And he ambled off in that loose, gangly way of a boy who'd grown too tall too fast and was unaccustomed to the length of his limbs.

I smiled after him, watching his blue-black pony-tail swinging in the crisp morning breeze. His gaunt, white face glinted in the moonlight as he approached his target.

In a little over a minute, he was back, smoke curling from the fag in his hand. He picked up the conversation where he'd left it. "The bus is sheduled to arrive at 7:10 or thereabouts so we've probably got a bit of a wait ahead o' us."

It was barely 6:00 a.m. I shivered again. The wind had picked up and it felt near freezing. I hoped the weather wasn't going to be uncharacteristically cold during my stay. The rain and mist I enjoyed, so long as the temperatures felt like spring.

"Maybe I'll go back and wait inside," I said. "It's chillier than I expected."

"Do that and you'll risk missin' the bus. It's often late, but can, just as easy, be early." Johnny took a long pull off his bummed cigarette. The white powder covering his face and the dark makeup smudged around his eyes gave him an Edward Scissorhands look and I wondered if the Irish girl he was meeting was goth too.

"Could be here any minute," he continued conversationally. "Or it might not come 'til 8:00."

"I say, you can't be serious."

The voice, speaking in a more cultured English accent than Johnny's cockney, came from behind me. I turned to see a dapper man, who looked to be somewhere in his mid to late sixties.

Dressed in a London Fog raincoat, he carried a black umbrella in one hand, and a smart, compact suitcase in the other. He reminded me immediately of the late

Patrick Macnee, known as John Steed in the 1960's British television series, *The Avengers*.

"Damned Irish, never could stick to a shedule." The Patrick Macnee look-a-like consulted his wristwatch.

"Well, I guess there's nothing for it, then." Turning his gaze to me, he said, "My dear, would you like to have a seat with me on that bench over there? You look a bit burdened under all those bags."

"That sounds like a good idea," I said, smiling. To Edward Scissorhands, I said, "Do you want to sit too, Johnny? Looks like there's room for three."

"Nah, fanks anyhow. Need to stretch me legs. 'Sides, all I got's this knapsack wif' me. Toofbrush and a change o' nickers.

"But the bloke's right," he said. "You look like you're carryin' the weight of the world on your shoulders." He gave me his now infamous gap-toothed grin, took another drag on his cig, and dismissed us both with a nod.

"The name's Preston Fortnight," said the dapper English gent, extending a gloved hand, and giving my mittened one a brisk shake. "You just head on over before someone else snags it up and I'll bring your bag along."

I opened my mouth to protest, not wanting this sophisticated man to have to drag my 50-pound suitcase with the wonky wheel to a bench several yards away, but he offered me a little half-smile and dismissed the gesture before I could speak. "Go on then. I'll be right along."

Even through my long underwear, the bench was like ice and I took in an involuntary gasp of air when my butt connected with its frosty surface. Preston's backside barely grazed the wooden planks before he was up and extending a hand to me to stand beside him.

"Oh, that won't do at all," he said, placing his suitcase on the bench and popping it open. With a flourish, he produced a neatly folded throw of dark gray wool, which he smoothed across the seat.

"There," he said. "That should do the trick." Turning once again to me, he bent slightly at the waist and, with a sweep of his hand, bad me to sit.

'Damn, I thought. 'He is totally John Steed! Mom, are you getting all this?' I silently asked my dead mother.

The Avengers was a television show we had shared from my childhood.

"I'll tell you what," Preston said, after I'd seated my freezing bum on the lovely thick covering of blanketed bench. "You stay here and watch for the bus and I'll go inside and get us each a coffee. What do you say?"

I peered up into his twinkling gray eyes. "That would be wonderful," I said as I reached for my fanny pack and the euros I'd tucked away inside it.

"No, no, my treat. You take milk and sugar, do you?"

"No, just black, thanks."

"Right then," and, tipping an imaginary hat, he was off to fetch the coffee.

Returning several minutes later, Preston Fortnight handed me my coffee and took his seat alongside me on the bench. "American, are you, Jennifer?" he asked, taking a tentative sip of his heavily milked coffee.

I tell him I am, and we chat a few minutes about where I've come from and where I'm headed. Then the conversation shifts to the life and times of Preston Fortnight.

"I was raised in a little village outside Greater Manchester. My mother was proper English, my father Dublin Irish." He offered a self-effacing chuckle. "A more unlikely union would be a challenge to find. Confusing for an only child, when one's parents are such opposites. It was always difficult to know just what was expected of me. Left me feeling a little like the odd shoe."

He took a long swallow of coffee, his eyes far away, gazing into the past. "Living in that house was like being raised by the sun and the moon. One all passion, fierce and hot one moment, and silly as summer the next. While the other was cool and distant as the stars above.

"The moon," he continued. "Otherwise known as my mother, was decisive; everything had a place and a plan. My father, that blazing orb of fire, never knew where he was going, but was always keen to get there."

He gave me a soft smile. "There I go, reminiscing like an old man. Of course, I am creeping up on my doddering years, you know."

"No," I said, eager to hear more. "Please go on. I want to hear about your life."

"Well, now," said Preston Fortnight, with a laugh and a pat on my knee. "I doubt even an Irish bus would be running late enough for you to hear all that."

"Then I'll settle for more about your childhood," I said, smiling back at him.

"You're being kind, but then I've always appreciated the kindness of strangers, and done my share of exploiting it as well!"

This time his smile reached his eyes, but it was a sad smile. "Now, my mother, there was another story. She was a proud woman and a bit hard. Never leaned on a soul in her life. My father never seemed to do anything but lean. Of course, that could be because he was usually drunk."

"That must have been hard for you," I said, taking a sip of my still scalding coffee. "Being so different from one another, I wonder what brought them together."

"Now, that one's easy." He grinned at me. "You're looking at the little fetal bonding agent as we speak. One careless escapade when my mother was little more than seventeen, and there they were...stuck with one another.

"Seventy years ago, a man, even a man like my father, didn't run away from his responsibilities the way men do in this day and age."

He chuckled, but it held no humor. "I don't believe either of them ever forgave me for it."

'Way to go, McCormack,' I thought. 'Walked right into that one.' But Preston appeared unperturbed.

"Ah, there's the bus, then. As me da would have said," he added, slipping easily into an Irish brogue, "May the Saints be praised." He gave me a wink and offered me his hand as we stood to gather our things and catch the bus.

Bus Layover and Auntie Angela's Hundred-Year-Old Mum

A little over two hours later, we arrived at the last stop-over before our final destination. The bus was far from full and I had the luxury of two seats to myself, one for me, and one for my backpack and computer bag that had, by that time, taken on tedious personalities of their own.

Falling instantly asleep, I regret that I missed almost all the scenery along the way. So far, my bus trip this year was a great deal less harrowing than the one the year before, had entailed three different bus stations, forcing me to haul two giant suitcases, backpack, and computer bag into and out of the baggage compartments of each...THREE TIMES.

Okay, 'nuff goin' on 'bout ancient history. On to me tale!

Preston Fortnight, ever the gentleman, caught up with me in time to take my bag from the baggage compartment below the bus and set it beside me on the sidewalk. We exchanged pleasant and, I hoped, heartfelt, goodbyes and he hailed a taxi and was out of my life.

I stood shivering in front of the Eireann Bus Station with the rest of the disheveled and glassy-eyed travelers.

One by one, the small crowd outside the station began to thin as one bus or another whisked them off to their varied destinations, none of which were mine. Soon, it was down to me, another woman about my age, and a young man with a boyish face, a sweet smile, and boarding school manners.

It had been 45 minutes since the bus had dropped us and I was growing a bit concerned. The bus station was closed, so there was no going inside to check the schedule. That was when I decided to interrupt the animated conversation going on between the woman and the sweet-faced young man.

"Oh yes," she said, offering me a cheerful smile. "There'll be a bus, all right. No frettin' o'er that. Afraid though 'tisn't scheduled to arrive 'til half-twelve."

It was now only 9:45. My warm knit cap filtered this disparaging news through a layer of fleece, effectively softening the blow.

"Auntie Angela," said the sweet-faced young man with the Harry Potter manners and an American accent. "Isn't there another bus line that might arrive sooner?"

"Well, there's the City Link just 'round that next bend." She pointed in the direction of the busy street.

"Maybe I should go check it out," said the young man. "It is Gran's hundredth birthday. I'd like to wish her a happy birthday while she's still among the living." He offered up a cheeky grin, and she gave his face a playful mittened slap.

"We'll have yer gran a good long time yet. I'm likely to go afore she does."

His grin broadened. "I'll run over to City Link and see if they have a bus running sooner than this one. If they do, I'll come back and get you both, and we can get out of this cold."

Auntie Angela and I stood in companionable silence while her nephew made the run to the next port in a storm. I think we were both too cold and worn out to make the effort at conversation. Moments later, he returned, flush-faced and out of breath.

"Come on, we've got to make a run for it. The bus is boarding now!"

"Did ye ask the driver to wait?"

Shaking his head, his face grim, Angela's nephew said, "He told me he can't hold it for us. He's on a strict schedule."

"Well, that's the biggest pile o' shite I've heard in a long time," came the bitter reply. "A strict schedule, my thistled arse."

"Come on, Auntie, you can gripe about him later. Right now, we've got to move if we're going to have any chance of making that bus."

With that, we loaded up and took off down the narrow, cobblestone street, our rolling bags bumping along behind us. And...we missed the bus, which was pulling away just as we reached the station.

"Damned bollox," Auntie Angela wheezed as she doubled over to catch her breath. "Did that on purpose, he did. Just to punish us fer takin' up wit' the competition. A strict schedule, my thistled arse."

A minute went by. Auntie Angela straightened and smiled, her good nature restored. "Be a luv, Mat'hew, an' find out when the next City Link bus leaves. We're here now, an' we're inside. We might as well give them our business as Eireann."

Dutifully, Matthew went to the ticket window to do as he was told.

Turning to me, Auntie Angela said, "Well, an' yer in a mite bit better shape than I am. I was the one holdin' up the party. Ye ran like the wind, ye did. As fast as Mat'hew. An', if ye dunna' mind me sayin', he's a mite bit younger than you an' I."

She gave me a wink. "But then again, ye Americans are into all that health an' fitness bollox, even payin' fees to torture chambers ye call gyms just so ye can fit into yer fancy New York clothes."

I made a point of looking down at my jeans and sweatshirt, then back up at Angela. "That's it," I said. "I'm nothing without my fashion."

To my delight and dismay, Auntie Angela tossed back her head and let out a guffaw that bounced off the walls of the nearly empty bus station. "An' yer quick too. Now, that's somethin' I appreciate."

Matthew returned from the ticket counter and the look on his face said it all. "The next bus isn't scheduled to arrive until 4:00 o'clock this afternoon."

"Shut yer mouth," Auntie Angela said, all good humor chased away by the desperate bad news. "Seems we canno' catch a bleedin' break fer tryin'. I guess we'll have to take our business back to Eireann, after all. But, mind ye, I'm no' runnin' full out an' riskin' a coronary. We can take our leisure."

Consulting the clock on the station wall, I said, "The bus doesn't come for another two and half hours. I might go find a breakfast place, get some coffee and a bite to eat. The two of you are welcome to join me if you'd like."

But before I'd even finished my sentence, Angela was shaking her head, looking woeful. "We canno' trust the bus wunna' be early. If we're away when it comes, we'll be bolloxed altogether.

"No, I'm afraid we're a right bit screwed. We wait in the cold wit' the hopes o' gettin' on the bus somewhere between now an' half-fourteen, er we find ourselves back here at City Link at sixteen hundred hours."

Matthew's face was crestfallen and I'm certain mine mirrored his. "Don't they ever stick to a schedule in Ireland?"

Offering up a bitter laugh, Auntie Angela said, "Only when they want to teach some gobshite a lesson."

After using the facilities to empty our bladders and make a futile attempt at freshening up, we trudged back to the Eireann Bus Station and huddled together on a cement bench outside.

After a few minutes of dejected silence, Matthew said brightly, "Auntie Angela, do you think it might be safe if I went in search of some breakfast food and coffee? I could bring it back here while you ladies wait for the bus?"

I prayed she would say yes. My prayer was answered.

Insisting this be my treat, I gave Matthew a 50-euro bill and we bade him God's speed as he went in search of a McDonalds. While he was away, Auntie Angela filled me in on the family history.

Here are the highlights: Angela is the youngest of 13 children born to Scottish born Angus McCloud and Irish Mary Margaret O'Shea. Old Angus died in his sleep a little over five years ago, but Mary Margaret, hearty Irish stock that she is, continues to go strong.

Living on her own in the wee cottage in which she raised her brood of 9 boys and 4 girls, Mary Margaret still runs the family farm, sheering the sheep each spring and selling the wool in the town square. "The wool's fer makin' ganseys an' jumpers an' such."

Angela's nearly 100-year-old mother relies on her hens for her eggs, her goats for her milk, and her lovingly tended vegetable patch for her produce. Accepting the fact that she's now a bit old for butchering her own cows, she, at last, has given the nod to the local butcher to supply her beef.

All but 4, counting Angela, of the 13 children have relocated to Boston. All are alive and well, with children and grandchildren of their own. The whole lot was journeying to Ireland for the birthday celebration to be held at a local pub this Tuesday next. And I'm invited! I wouldn't miss it for the world.

CHAPTER 3

Arrived!

The apartment, only two long blocks from the bus stop, was spacious and lovely, with two bedrooms, two baths, and a fully outfitted kitchen. The patio doors look out over the harbor, where anchored fishing boats bob in the rolling waters and gale force winds of Ireland's Wild Atlantic Way.

The only drawback was the steep series of stone steps leading down to the door and the only way in and out. I set my 50-pound suitcase at the top of the steps, gave it a swift kick, and watched its awkward somersault descent.

CHAPTER 4

Fishermen at Work

It was a lovely morning, with mild temperatures and an overcast sky. Heading east from my apartment, I took a winding road that ran alongside the harbor. A long line of fishing boats, small and large, were docked and waiting to be loaded and launched.

Whether it be three men in a dingy or ten men on a heavily rigged fishing vessel, the work is backbreaking and often treacherous. The men's faces are ruddy and weathered from wind and rain. The lines around their eyes are etched there from months and years spent scanning sea and sky like gypsies reading tea leaves.

I have yet to spot a female on the deck of a fishing boat. My guess is that this is more an issue of practicality than sexism. The men, manning the nets and loading the massive coolers and equipment onto the boats, embody the stereotype of the burly fisherman.

Big men, not always tall, but thick, with big hands and sturdy limbs, hoist heavy anchors on massive links of chain, crusted and green from soaking in seawater, up from the depths, to prepare for the launch. Rough ropes in complex knots are undone from the dock and reeled in to lay in dripping heaps of coil in a corner of the boat.

Watching this up close can be mesmerizing, and I leaned on the wall of the stone bridge above the churning water, taking in the preparations for the day's fishing. The fishermen, a friendly lot, traded banter across boats as they readied their rigs for the sea. Wool hats pulled low over foreheads, round faces cracking into grins that rippled outward from the corners of their mouths to the lobes of their wool capped ears, the effect like that of a stone dropped into a pool of still water.

On occasion, one or another of the men would look up at me, offer a brief wave and holler "Hiya Missus," their voices carrying above the roar of the wind. And always I waved back, delighted to be included in the ritual of their daily lives.

"An' yer a new face 'round here." A man with bright green eyes in a chapped, red face came to stand beside me.

"Yes," I said, turning to face him and feeling the bracing wind push my hair away from my face. "I just arrived yesterday."

He cocked his head to one side and examined me. "American, are ye?"

"Yes," I said as the wind became a gale that stole my breath.

"On holiday, are ye?"

Again, I answered in the affirmative.

"From where 'bouts do ye hale in America?"

"Michigan."

"Aye, I know it some. Snows a lot, does it, in Michigan? An' bitter cold this time o' year, if I remember me geography."

Again, I nodded, the wind pushing the words back down my throat.

"Ye appreciate the work we do here," he said. "I can see it written in yer face. Plain as day there in yer eyes. That's a good thing an', if ye dunna' mind me sayin', a rare one in my experience."

Seeing I was having trouble braving the gale, he walked around me and leaned on the wall to my other side, allowing me to turn my back to the howling wind.

I smiled my thanks, found my breath and my voice enough to respond. "You're a fisherman?"

"Aye, dun this work all me life, as did me da afore me, his afore him, an' so on down the line."

"It's daunting to me, the work you do," I said as my eyes strayed from his to a mid-sized boat just visible in the lapping waters over his left shoulder.

On the boat, one man stood, working, hand over hand, to bring in the long chain of anchor. Another bent, one foot on the deck of the swaying ship, the other on the dock, as he untied the thick knot of rope that lashed it to the post.

It was amazing to me how he managed to keep his balance. It was like watching a real-life ballet unfold before my eyes.

The fisherman beside me turned to see what had captured my attention, watched with me a moment, and then turned back. "Is it the physical labor then, that ye find dauntin'?"

I nodded, shifting my gaze back to him. His eyes narrowed against the wind and I could see he was assessing me. I found myself thinking he would make a good detective. Hmm...retired fishing boat captain turned private investigator. Has potential.

Bringing myself back to the conversation, I said, "It's that, yes. The strength and stamina it takes to do this kind of work, day in and day out, is something I cannot even begin to imagine.

"But it's more than that. It's the fact that, every single day, you venture out on the ocean to face whatever nature has in store."

He continued to study me with those narrowed green eyes, his face sober, though his mouth and jaw were relaxed.

I took a breath. "The fact that you go out on the water each and every morning, never knowing if you'll be coming home again each night, never knowing for certain if you'll step foot again on dry land. It's that uncertainty, that lack of guarantee, that I think I find most daunting."

At this, he broke into a wide grin. "Oh, is that all, then?" He laughed, dissolving the assessing stare. "Well, Missus, ain't none o' us got any guarantees in this life. Ye've lived long 'nuff, surely, to be plain aware o' that."

I grinned back, laughing with him. "You're right on that score," I said. "It's just that, for most of us, for me for sure, I can hide that fact from myself pretty nicely. I can bury the uncertainty of life and death beneath the mundane routine of everyday life."

"An' what is it ye think we do?" With a sweep of his hand, he took in the panorama of men and boats, nets and lines and rigging. "We, each o' us, from the fisherman to the shop clerk to the barman to the woman on holiday, face down death each an' every day, knowin' it'll get us, each an' every one o' us, sure as Shannon, in the end."

CHAPTER 5

Long Walks and the Encounters Therein

3 Brief Tales

A Peeing Yapper Ruins It for the Rest of Us

In my wanderings, I came to a Catholic Church. Ancient and imposing, it towered above me and I was swallowed in its shadow. Posted on the front gate was the message:

NO DOGS ALLOWED IN PEWS:
By order of Father Donovan.

"An' it's a right shame, it is," offered a man's voice from behind me.

I whirled around to see a lovely looking man, with sparkling blue eyes and a tumble of dark curls that framed a handsome face and chiseled features.

"Oh, hello," I said, a bit breathless with surprise and, well... surprise.

"The priest's proclamation, there," he said, inclining his head toward the sign. "A little yapper peed in an American woman's handbag at the height o' the tourist season last year, so dogs are now relegated to the back o' the church. So, ye know, of a Sunday, that's where I've parked me arse, e'er since that fateful day."

"Because you want to sit with your dog?"

"Well, that, sure, and because I am one," the gorgeous man said, a twinkle in his eye.

"I dunna' know ye from Joe Soap."

long my walk, a man approached me.

"No, dunna' speak," he said, putting a finger to his lips. "I'm after livin' in this village me whole life, an' I dunna' know ye from Joe Soap. So, I'm figurin' ye must be a stranger to these parts. I want to guess, by the look o' ye, where yer from."

With that, he stepped back and took me in from head to toe, his eyes narrowed in appraisal. After a moment's scrutiny, he said, "County Kerry's me guess, up Carrig Way?"

I smiled and shook my head.

"Fuck, an' I'm usually good at this. No, dunna' be after tellin' me, now. Let me have another go."

I nodded, giving him a grin.

"County Clare then, up Shannon way?"

Offering an apologetic smile, I shook my head.

At this, he dropped his eyes and examined my blue jeans and sneakers. "Well, fuck me sideways, yer no' from Ireland at all, am I right on that?"

I nodded, my smile becoming a full-out grin.

"A'course, an' what was I thinkin'? I must a'been bleedin' daft. The cut o' yer clothes isna' Irish at all. So, an' as it changes the entire game then, ye must grant me another try."

Inclining my head, I gave him the okay.

"Aye, an' I'll get it yet, I will. Just see if I don't." He made a show of stroking his chin in contemplation.

"Well now, let's see 'bout this," and proceeded to think aloud. "Yer no' English, an' that's fer sure. On account o' ye dunna' look like ye got a stick up yer arse.

"And ye havena' the demeanor o' the Eastern European. Fer one thing, ye got nowhere on ye to be hidin' yer Uzi. An' ye dunna' look like yer after clickin' yer heels an' givin' me a salute.

"I'm doubtin' yer Canadian. Just a feelin' I have, based on nuthin' in particular, so I could be off 'bout that. Which leaves American."

He gave a long, slow shake of his head. "An' that's dafter than all me guesses put together. There's no way yer after bein' an American; ye've kept yer mouth shut fer way too long."

Mad Casey and Molly Molloy

The weather was mild, so I decided to go for a walk along the docks and up into the winding countryside that paralleled the shoreline. About twenty minutes into my walk, I came to a beautiful stone house, with a massive bay window overlooking the water, and stopped to take some pictures. As I was snapping away, a woman and her dog, a sweet tempered yellow lab, rounded the bend behind me and stopped to say hello.

"Are ye the American woman after buyin' this place, then?" she asked, her expression all sorts of inquisitive.

"Oh no," I said. "I just thought it was beautiful and decided to take some pictures."

"Aye, an' that it is," the woman nodded as I cuddled and cooed over her big friendly dog. "I canno' find a single soul in town whose met her, an' we're all gettin' 'bout ready to burst wit' curiosity," she said. "I'm sorry yer no' her. Ye look like a nice person."

"Thanks," I said, offering her a smile as the dog extended a muddy paw for me to shake. "People are so friendly here, you make it easy to be nice."

She stared down at me, a wry smile tugging at the corner of her mouth. "No' many would shake me Molly Molloy's paw when it's covered in mud an' muck."

I grinned back at her, holding the dog's giant, dripping paw in my hand. "I think it would be rude not to take a lady's hand when she offers it."

The woman tossed back her head and laughed. "Yer obviously no' the American who bought this house. If ye had been, the whole town woulda' known ye by now. I'm Madeline Casey. But ye can call me Mad; every'un else does.

"No, it's true 'nuff," she said, as though I'd protested. "Just ask any'un, an' they'll be after tellin' ye, there goes Mad Casey now, goin' ninety to the duzzen, wit' her double mad dog chasin' after."

"It's nice to meet you," I said and meant it as I looked up into her sparkling hazel eyes. Mad Casey is an attractive woman, probably in her late thirties, with a pert nose, an infectious grin, and shoulder length auburn hair swept away from her face with a purple headband. I introduced myself and added, "You and your dog have fantastic names."

"Thanks, an' it's nice to meet ye too, Jennifer," she said as I pulled myself up from my crouch, wiped my now muddy hand on my jeans and offered it to her. She gave it a brisk, no-nonsense shake. "Molly here is named after me grandmother on me father's side. I wanted to keep me name when I married Sean Casey, but the fuckin' gobshite had such a fit o'er it, in the end I had to give in. So, Molly's the one's got to carry it on.

"So, where ye from, Jennifer?"

"Michigan, in the United States."

"An' what house are ye after buyin'?"

"Oh, I'm just here on holiday, though I think I might love living here."

"So, an' ye should do it, Woman," Mad Casey said, her tone matter-of-fact. "Ye'd be an asset to us, I can tell that already. Any person that's after appreciatin' me Molly

48

Molloy full on, the way ye have, has somethin' special to offer."

I smiled. "You and Molly Molloy are very sweet."

Surprising me, she wouldn't let it go. "So, tell me real like, what's keepin' ye from gettin' the fuck out o' America and comin' here to live? Dunna' tell me yer in favor o' that fecker o' a new president?"

"Oh no, Trump would not be a reason for me to stay in the States," I said, no longer smiling.

"Then what is it that's holdin' ye back? Is it yer man, then? He wouldna' want to join ye here in Ireland?"

My grin was back in place. "He might take some convincing."

"Aye, but ye could do it. How could he turn down them eyes? Men are simple creatures. Just slide yer hand down his pants an' give it a right good squeeze. Trust me, he'll foller ye anywhere."

"I'll have to try that," I said, and we were laughing again.

Just as I thought we were about to part ways, Mad Casey surprised me by coming back yet again to the subject of moving to Ireland. "Is it yer job, then? Ye look like a resourceful woman. Ye could find a way. What is it yer after doin' fer work?"

"I'm a psychologist."

"Well, an' there ye go. Ye just met yer first patient. An' there's plenty more where I come from.

"There, an' it's settled. We'll go house huntin' tomorrow." She leaned in, gave me a kiss on the cheek and she and Molly Molloy were off, racing up the road ahead.

Calling back over her shoulder, she said, "Everybody knows everybody in this village. Ye decide to take me up on me offer, just ask any'un and they'll direct ye."

CHAPTER 6

On Getting Lost

2 More Encounters

A Loooooong Walk

harmed by my encounter with Mad Casey and Molly Molloy, I continued my walk along the curving roadway and up into the hills. To my right, were cottages with welcoming arched doors painted in glossy primary colors to match the trim. Beneath tiny square windows, flowerboxes overflowed with hardy perennials that could withstand the cold winds coming in off the sea.

On my left, was a knee-high rock wall. On the other side of the wall was a sloping hill of rock and moss, lichen, and sprigs of grass, scrub, and thistle in a chaotic tumble down to the sea. The view was spectacular. And majestic. And strong. And lonely.

The personality of the Connemara landscape feels hard and lean, and, like the people who live here, stoic. Don't misunderstand me, the Wild Atlantic Way foams up around any fishing village and will sweep a fisherman overboard just as fast in each. It's the attitude of the land and rock and people that determines the difference between the emerald coast and the rugged Connemara.

As I walked, the clouds began to gather in the blue of the sky, dimming the sunny afternoon, only to reveal it again in a brilliant, blinding reprieve a few seconds later. Sheep, cows, and herding dogs roamed the hillside.

I came to a narrow road of moss and stone. The tiny road wound uphill and then down and then up again, before coming to an end, where it intersected with another, wider road.

On the edge of this wider road was a brown road sign written in Gaelic with arrows pointing in opposite directions. Sadly, I cannot read Gaelic and it is one of those languages where the educated guess flunks the test every time. Stumped about which way to turn, I followed my instincts and went left.

Unfortunately, my directional instincts are often wrong. For a long time, I went the wrong way. For a long time, I went the wrong way. For a long time, I went the wrong way. The going the wrong way part is hardly new to me, so I understood and accepted the distinct possibility that I was walking away from the village rather than toward it. Oh well, at least the sun was shining.

Weather on an island, in the middle of the ocean, can change in an instant, and this was precisely what it did. Clouds rolled in, dark and thunderous. A moment later, the heavens opened, unleashing the tears of a thousand years of Irish heartache.

Sheets of rain pummeled my head and shoulders with steely bullets of icy water, soaking my hair and running in rivers down my back under the collar of my down vest. The rain was pounding me so hard that I had trouble keeping my eyes clear to see where I was going.

Cars barreled passed, spraying me with bog water that had begun to bubble up out of ruts in the road. The few houses I could see were dark and void of life. Head down, I kept walking, hoping beyond hope I was going the right way.

Another several minutes went by. It felt like an hour. A car, small but sturdy, came toward me, slowed, and turned into the driveway of a cheerful yellow cottage surrounded by a black wrought iron fence.

The woman in the driver's seat tugged her slicker up over her head as she stepped from the car onto the stone path leading to the bright orange door. The passenger door and both back doors flew open and children of all sizes, four of them, tumbled out.

The woman raised her hand in a friendly wave and splashed through the mud and water in her wellies to the gate to meet me.

"Excuse me," I said, projecting my voice over the roar of the rain. "I'm trying to get back to town. Am I going in the right direction?"

"Oh no, no' at all, yer not," She said, managing to sound both cheerful and empathetic in that unique way I have only encountered here in Ireland. "The village is a mad sight down that way." She pointed in the direction from which I had been trudging for the last 45 minutes. "It's three miles er more to Town Centre."

I offered her a weak smile.

"I'd be after givin' ye a lift, I would, but I'm goin' to be busy murderin' me children."

Said children, three boys whose ages looked to be 7, 10, and 13, and a little girl of about 6, were busy slugging one another in the head and chest, the little girl shoving the full weight of her compact little body into each brother in turn, sending them sprawling into the mud.

I looked back at the woman and nodded. "Understood. Thanks for putting me back on track."

"Afore ye head," she said, touching my sodden sleeve with the tip of one finger. "Any advice on how I ought go 'bout doin' 'em in?"

One by one, I studied the group of hooligans, now covered from head to toe in dripping muck. "I think I'd take the big one out first." I indicated the gangly 13-year-old boy who was, at that moment, swinging the youngest of his brothers by the ankles, attempting, I think, to use the younger boy's body as his weapon of choice in hurling the two remaining ruffians into outer space. "He looks like he might give you the most trouble."

"Brilliant," she said. "I'll take yer advice an' ye take mine an' ye'll be back to town in time fer supper."

The Irish Good Samaritan

The enchanted Connemara views mesmerized me, and before I knew it, I had walked for nearly two hours along the winding coast and up into the hills. The fine mist and warm temperature felt like spring. The wind had died down and I was soaking up the solitude of the brilliant and melancholy landscape that surrounded me.

After a while, even the mist stopped. Though the sun never broke through the furrowed brow of clouds, the day grew dry as well as warm and the birdsong was magnificent. The farther I went, the incline grew steeper and the view more spectacular.

I continued to make my way up the curving road, meeting the occasional car, walker, or person on a bicycle. Dogs too, loads of them, mostly of the herding variety, and all of them gentle and sweet and usually attached to a person who was coming along behind them.

Sheep were everywhere, grazing on the slopes and in the valleys, some even snuffling at the bare sprigs of grass poking with stubborn determination through cracks in the pavement. Cows and horses dotted the landscape in every direction. Deep in rugged ravines, chickens pecked and scrabbled beside the wild birds.

When they use the term "Free Range" in Ireland, it truly means Free Range, not "I'll let you out of your cage for 15 minutes twice a day," as we've come to understand it in the US.

Just a little under 2 hours into my walk, the brooding sky opened. Torrents of hard rain poured down, drenching me instantly and utterly. The breathtaking vistas I had been enjoying were now nothing but a watery blur. And I was a long, long way from home.

The wind had picked up and, turning back in the direction I had come, I was walking right into it...downhill. Good thing me tennies got good grippers on the bottoms o' 'em! The rain felt like pebbles slamming into my face and I had to squint to protect my eyes.

Being more experienced judges than I of the changing weather, the people I'd met on the road had gone inside to their nice cozy turf fires prior to the onslaught and I was alone. Even the sheep, chickens, cows, and horses were safely tucked away.

Reflecting on it later, I realized I had noticed the working dogs nosing the larger animals in from the pastures about a half an hour before the rain began. Note to self: When you see that happening, head back!

I'd walked down no more than one lonely, soggy hill when a car coming toward me, pulled to a stop. Behind the wheel was an ancient little man, tufts of gray fuzz popping out from beneath his checked cap.

He rolled down the window. "Stayin' in the village, are ye?" he asked, peeping out from under his cap. His was a small, aged face, and his eyes were black dots set deep in the crinkled skin.

"I am," I said as I shielded my face from the rain with the curve of my hand.

"Well, get in an' I'll take ye back." This was delivered as a statement, in a weary voice, as though he'd done it many times before.

"Are you sure?" I asked, raising my voice to be heard above the roar of the wind. "I don't want to take you out of your way."

"Well," he said, with a shrug. "Yer wastin' me time arguin' 'bout it now, ain't ye? Get on in an' I'll take ye home."

I did.

Side Note: *In case you're concerned over my sudden penchant for hitch hiking, please rest assured that I only accept rides from kindly looking women or little old men who weigh less than I do.*

Climbing in, I apologized for the advanced state of my waterlogged, self and again thanked him for his kindness in offering the ride.

"No bother," he replied, waving away my sentiment. "Ye dunna' want to be caught out in this nasty shite."

After that, except for the drip-drip-drip of my wet coat and hair on his cloth upholstery and the steady slap of the wipers on the windscreen, we rode in silence.

When he spoke again, the sound startled me out of my wet reverie. "Yeah, an' I passed ye on me way into the village this mornin'. A surprise it was to see ye way up at the top o' the road on me way home.

"Then when ye spoke, an' I realized ye was an American. Well, ye 'bout knocked me out o' me knickers.

"The Irish'll walk that far, an' sometimes other Europeans, but no' too often will ye find an American willin' to do it. No' unless they'd be all topped out in them million-dollar hiking uniforms, an' carryin' 'nuff supplies on their backs fer a 10-day trip into the wilderness."

I laughed. "I really wasn't intending to walk that far. It was just such a mild day and so beautiful, I lost track of how far I was going."

"Well," he mused, more to himself than to me. "Part o' me says yer a bleedin' eejit. Another part o' me's feelin' a wee bit o' respect. To see ye trudgin' back the way ye come, head down an' grim, sort o' touched me heart."

Laughing, I said, "Being a bleeding idiot, I don't think I had much choice."

"True, true," he said, stroking his chin as he took the curve into town. "Somethin' in the way ye were walkin', both on the way up an' the way down, told me ye weren't 'bout to go cryin' in yer beer o'er it though, an' that's a good thing.

"Ye must have some Irish blood. Eejit 'nuff to get yerself into the mess, but stoic 'nuff to get yerself out again wit'out a mess o' bitchin' an' complainin'."

He dropped me in town, gave a single wave, and was gone.

CHAPTER 7

Time to meet the Village Barkeeps

6 Illustrative Stories

The barkeeps in the segments that follow are truly the unsung heroes of this little village, at least for me they were, as you will discover upon reading a couple of my other adventures that occurred later in the month.

Barkeep Rory Rolls the Dice
on a Joke

n this particular evening, I stopped in at a pub I'd only visited once before. Rory, the barkeep, is a gentle, soft spoken soul, and I find his presence comforting.

I looked up from my Jamie's and Ginger to see Rory eyeing me, his expression impossible to read. At last, he said, "I'm tryin' to make up me mind 'bout whether er no' to share a funny you-tube video wit' ye.

"It's no' goin' to be to everyone's taste, an' I'm no' after knowin' yer sense o' humor an' preferences."

I assured him I was a pretty good audience for most kinds of humor.

"Ye might be offended."

I grinned. "It takes a lot to offend me."

Grinning back, Rory nodded. "An' that's the way ye seem to me."

Slapping the bar with the flat of one hand, he said, "Okay, I'll take a chance an' show it to ye. Ye'll either laugh so hard, ye'll come close to pissin' yerself, er ye'll flounce out o' me bar, all bristles an' starch, an' I'll na'er see the likes o' ye again."

Producing his phone from beneath the bar, he brought up the video.

If you'd like to see it for yourself, Google: Jesus Crosses the Road to the song I Will Survive by Gloria Gaynor. For me, this was the beginning of a beautiful friendship with yer man Rory.

The Two Stool Rule

This story, more observational in nature, isn't about the barkeep, though colorful anecdotes on that score are upcoming. My favorite pub in town is a little hole in the wall favored by locals. Only men at the bar, most of them fishermen. Friendly enough and unassuming, though not much for 'waggin' their tongues.'

Once they got over the initial shock of seeing a woman plunk her arse down on one of the bar stools, they were fine to offer the traditional, "Hiya Missus."

My habit is to climb onto a barstool at about 1:00 p.m. Don't worry, I haven't started drinkin' me Jamie's an' Ginger quite that early in the day, though if ye gave me 'nuff time here, I just might.

In the early afternoons, the patrons generally consist of three older men, all somewhere, according to the pub's owner Tom, between the ages of eighty-three and a hundred-and-thirty-seven. Two of these men are retired fishermen. The third is a retired pharmacist who was "by way o' ownin' the apothecary just 'round the bend. Owned an' operated for o'er 60 years."

While these men will exchange brief pleasantries with me when I invade their afternoon sanctuary, they remain reticent to share more. And eye contact is absolutely out of the question. Barkeep Dermot (nickname to be revealed in the next story), however, is always willing to fill the silence in funny and entertaining ways.

An unspoken rule, in operation only in the hours between 1:00 and 3:00 p.m., is something I have dubbed The Two Stool Rule.

It goes like this: A distance of two bar stools on either side of the American woman must be maintained at all times when seated at the bar. Being the only woman I've yet to encounter at this pub makes it so far impossible to ascertain whether this rule came into existence for my benefit or if it is standard practice. In the US it might be better recognized as the Assured Clear Distance rule.

The New Baldy Jesus

One early Saturday evening, I walked into the pub of the Two Stool Rule to find four men I hadn't before encountered. Three sat side by side, two howling with laughter at something the third had just said. The fourth, an ancient man bearing an eerie resemblance to a sea turtle, sat in silence at the opposite end of the bar. Of the barkeep, there was no sign.

"Oh, an' I'm afraid it's strictly self-service tonight," said the one who'd sent his mates into a fit of guffaws.

"Aye," said one of the other two, once his laughter had subsided. "We dunna' know what happened to Big Jesus there who normally tends the bar." The barkeep's name is Dermot, but the patrons often refer to him as Big Jesus (Big: in reference to his over 6-foot height and broad-shouldered frame, Jesus: in reference to his beard and long flowing hair).

"Disappeared wit'out a trace, he did," said the first.

Rounding the bar, the third man positioned himself opposite me. "Can I pour ye a pint then, Missus?"

I smiled and said, "That would be very nice of you, but I'm afraid I'm not a beer drinker."

"Ah, no bother," the man said. "Just as long as yer no' requirin' any o' them fancy umbreller drinks ye have in America er on them tropical islands, we should be okay."

His mates on my side of the bar were having a grand time laughing and teasing their friend about being the "Second Coming o' the new Baldy Jesus."

Grinning, I requested my Jameson's and Ginger Ale.

"Jaimie's an' Ginger, comin' up fer the lovely wee lassie." And he set it before me on the bar.

It was then the barkeep lumbered out from the back room. "I rushed out o' the toilet when I heard a girlie voice behind me bar," he said, referring to the man tending bar in his absence.

Spotting me, his eyebrows shot up and his face flushed a deep red. "Oh, an' wouldna' ye know, there is a girlie at the bar. Honest, an' I wasna' talkin' 'bout ye," he said, offering me a sheepish grin. "I was actin' the maggot wit' Timot'y o'er there. I'd no idea there'd be an actual woman sittin' at me bar."

"An' the reason fer that," said the first man. "Is no woman has graced the likes o' this bar in well on thirty years."

"No' true," said Dermot, the barkeep. "This wee lass was in just a few days back. An' Ole Baldy Frank swaggered o'er an' was talkin' the shite to her all about his great knowledge o' Americans an' how useless they all are."

This bit was in reference to a minor interaction that occurred my first night in town and one which I didn't consider entertaining enough to include in my series of stories.

"Couldna' take a sip o' her Jamie's an' Ginger wit'out him goin' off 'bout Americans this an' Americans that. Poor girlie didna' stand a chance."

"Well, an' ye can come back here anytime," said the Big Jesus stand-in. By then, he'd returned to his seat on the patrons' side of the bar. "We'll protect ye from the likes o' Ole' Baldy Frank, we will."

"Aye," croaked the sea turtle propped against the Beamish tap. "An' who's goin' to protect her from the likes o' us?"

The Russian at the Bar

My evening began at 6:00 with a single shot of Powers whiskey and enjoyable chatter at the bar over which Big Jesus presided. A few minutes after I took my seat at the bar, a young man came in and plunked down next to me.

Big Jesus: "What can I get ye?"

Young man replied in broken English: "I take Guinness."

Big Jesus: "A pint then?"

Young man: "Da."

Big Jesus pulled him his pint and set it on the bar in front of him. The young man struggled to count out coins for the beer. Big Jesus helped by selecting the correct ones from the young man's open palm. Then the young man turned to me.

Young man: "You are beautiful woman. I only here one day and they make me go back Russia. Come, have sex with me. I make you more satisfied den you ever been in yoor life."

Big Jesus's expressive eyebrows shot up. I shook my head, politely declined, and moved several stools down until I was sitting nearly on top of two old fishermen huddled together at the corner of the bar. The young Russian picked up his beer and followed me, pulling his bar stool in close until I could feel (and smell) his hot breath on my neck.

Young man: "No, I heart attack serious. I give you time of yoor life. You gon' want that when come time you die."

I wasn't sure just what he meant by this. Was he waxing philosophical? Was he referencing my advanced age? Was he letting me know that, after rocking my world, he was planning to kill me?

Big Jesus had followed the young Russian, who had followed me, down to the corner of the bar, eyebrows still perched in the rafters of his giant forehead. The fishermen had stopped talking and had turned their ruddy faces to the young man now complacently sipping his pint.

Again, I shook my head and declined the invitation.

Big Jesus, as did the fishermen, turned to see what the Russian's next move might be. They looked like they were watching a tennis match.

Young man: "I tell you is true. I may no' look (pronounced like Luke) like much, but I promise you, I good (pronounced like Gouda without the a). You no regret."

Before I could decline a third time, Big Jesus took the reins.

Big Jesus: "Listen friend, ye dunna' want to be messin' wit' this one. Total nut job, she is."

Young man: "Wha'?

Big Jesus, nodding: "Absolutely, fuckin' mental. Fuckin' criminally insane, she is."

Young man, a crease appearing in his smooth, young brow: "I no' understand."

Big Jesus: "I'm tellin' ye this fer yer own good, Man. She's no' the full shillin'. Ye havena' got a baldy wit' her. The woman's mean an' crazy. Steal the sugar right out o' yer tea, she would."

Now, he was just showing off. The young man had no more idea of the message coming his way than had Big Jesus addressed him in an ancient Egyptian dialect. The young Russian, however, did appear to have hit a speed bump in his road to conquest.

Big Jesus rolled up the sleeve of his checked shirt, exposing an old, but nasty scar that ran the outer length of his right forearm from wrist bone to elbow. "Ye see this scar?" He pointed to the pink, puckered mass of twisted tissue.

The young Russian nodded, eyes glued to the scar.

Big Jesus nodded toward me: "Want to know how I got this scar?"

The young Russian nodded.

Big Jesus: "*She* gave me this scar."

The ruddy-faced fishermen were having a hard time keeping their faces straight, but they needn't have worried; the young Russian had eyes only for the scar.

"Ye see," Big Jesus said, "We used to go out like. No' anymore, a'course. A bit too much o' a mentaller. I had to get out.

"A'course, I didna' know that until it was almost too late. Anyway, she come in here one night, caught me chattin' up another girl. Came at me wit' a butcher knife, she did."

The young Russian's eyes grew wide. I decided maybe he understood more of Big Jesus's words than I'd previously believed.

Big Jesus: "Ye see, this here," he said, tracing the line of the scar with the tip of an index finger. "Is what ye'd call a defensive wound, er so the Garda said when they came to break it up. I was just tryin' to keep me beautiful face from bein' marked fer life. But I'll tell ye, wasna' no'un in this bar bettin' on me. Isna' that right, boys?" He turned to the fishermen who nodded and grumbled their agreement, not trusting themselves to meet the young Russian's eye.

Big Jesus: "Take me advice, Man, an' stay away from this one. She'll gouge out yer eyes, pop 'em in her mouth, an' wash 'em down wit' her Powers."

Big Jesus nodded to my drink. "An' that's if ye do satisfy her. If ye dunna' satisfy, then only God himself can save yer sorry arse. An' ye na'er know when even He might turn his tail and run."

Lifting himself from the barstool, the young Russian turned and bolted for the door, a half pint of Guinness abandoned on the bar.

Barkeep Psychologist and a Grieving Kathleen

O n a side street sits a quiet pub, equipped with a front room bar, seating area, and a peat burning fireplace. Another set of wooden doors leads from the front room to another, larger room furnished more as a restaurant, with a number of tables and booths, a pool table, another, longer bar, and two peat burning fireplaces.

This night, I chose to take a seat at the front room bar, a few stools down from the pub's one other patron, a woman in a cloth coat and dark head scarf. She wore brown pants that looked to be made of a coarse material and a pair of sturdy work boots, also brown, and laced to the ankle. Bent over a pint of dark beer, often referred to by the Irish as black stuff, she and the barkeep Sime (pronounced Sheem) engaged in quiet conversation.

Sime acknowledged me with the customary Irish wink but didn't immediately break away from the woman. Foreheads nearly touching, voices no more than a mumble, the two continued what looked to be a serious dialogue, an uncommon occurrence in my Irish experience. I wondered if I ought to vacate this bar for the one behind door number two.

As if reading my thoughts, or more likely, the subtle shift in my body language, Sime's eyes slid my way and he gave an almost imperceptible shake of his head. It was enough to keep me in my seat. The woman hadn't appeared to notice me at all.

She was older than I had originally thought, with a gaunt profile and prominent hooked nose. Deep vertical lines ran from the corner of her eye to her mouth. Scalloped skin hung loose along her jaw.

Misery was etched in the paper-thin skin around her eye. The downward turn of her mouth spoke of mountainous pain and oceans of sadness. Even so, the quiet, but intense dialogue and the tenderness in Sime's eyes told me she was not, by nature, a dweller in misery. Something had happened to this woman. Something had ravaged her.

Another moment passed before they broke apart. Sime moved down the bar toward me, a broad smile washing the somber expression from everything but his eyes.

"Hiya, Jennifer. Will it be Jamie's an' Ginger, er do ye want to go wit' the Diet 7Up?"

"I'll do the Diet 7Up this time, Sime. Thanks."

The woman's face pivoted on her too-thin neck until she was facing me. It was eerie, almost reptilian, the way the rest of her body remained facing the bar and only her narrow head turned. Her eyes were small and dark, like shiny beads, in the pub's dim light, and the hook nose put me in mind of a bird of prey. I was unnerved yet fascinated.

I smiled and said hello. Not returning the greeting, she studied me in silence. Again, I had the uncanny sense of a mouse caught in the sights of a hawk.

Setting my drink on the bar in front of me, Sime said, "Jennifer, this is Kat'leen Muldoon. Kat'leen, this is Jennifer, a writer visitin' from America. She's goin' to write a novel set in Ireland. She's other credits to her name, if ye'd care to know them."

Kathleen Muldoon, speaking to Sime, continued to stare at me, her head cocked at that unnatural angle. Her voice rasped, like cobwebs draping her vocal chords. "Writers

80

are a penny a pound 'round here," she said, her face expressionless. "I'd care to know the other credits."

This was a Twilight Zone experience if ever I'd had one, and I could feel my smile slipping, but I was way too intrigued to scuttle away now.

Side Note: *Sime is a natural historian. His presentation is that of a kindly professor. My conversations with Sime are always interesting and there seems no limit to his knowledge.*

Not only is Sime well versed in Irish history, he pays attention to the political, cultural, and sociological climate of all parts of the world. In addition, he exudes patience and is a remarkable listener. In these ways, he reminds me of the fisherman I met on the docks a couple of weeks before, the one out of which I may fashion a detective. Hmmm...perhaps our detective could use a walking encyclopedia sidekick?

Okay, back to Kathleen Muldoon:

Sime said, "Jennifer practices psychology in America. She works wit' people when traumatic things happen to them. She works wit' people who are grievin', an' helps them to heal their broken hearts."

Kathleen's eyebrows moved fractionally upward. Otherwise, her expression did not change.

Sime went on. "An' here's another interestin' bit. In her spare time, she does ghost trackin'."

"Do ye have the second sight?" Kathleen's cobwebby voice demanded to know.

"No," I said, encouraged by the fact that she was, at last, addressing me directly. "At least I don't think so. I have a lot of curiosity about life after death, and sometimes I like to see if I can gather evidence that could point to the existence of consciousness beyond physical death."

"And have ye had success?"

"Some, yes."

"An' so ye know it to be true," she offered with a single nod of her fragile head. "Help Sime close the bar some night, an' that'll teach ye, if nuthin' else does. Here in Ireland, we na'er doubted it fer a minute. Tis only the Americans question somethin' so obvious as that."

Smiling, I acknowledged the truth in her statement.

Sime broke in, "Kathleen, I think Jennifer might do ye some good if she's willin'. Would ye mind if I told her yer story?"

"Aye, an' ye can," Kathleen said, surprising me. "No' much o' a story, least nuthin' others havena' gone through as well, but go ahead, if ye must."

"Kathleen's husband Seamus died a couple o' weeks back, an' she's havin' a brutal time o' it," Sime said, his voice warm, yet matter-of-fact. "Might help if she could talk it out a bit wit' someone trained as yerself."

This was a brand new grief, no time for even a thin layer of skin to grow over the wound. It was clear to me this woman was still bleeding, her heart shattered to bits. I could certainly spend time talking with her here in this pub, but she would need so much more than I was in a position to give.

I'd known from talking with Sime a few days before, that the nearest therapist was more than an hour and 45 minutes away. There was no way this woman was about to travel so far to see a therapist. I doubted she'd do it if one hung up a shingle just down the street. Sime was her shrink and I was glad and grateful he was there.

I expressed condolences that always feel too hollow, and Kathleen surprised me yet again by abandoning her barstool and coming to sit next to me.

Her eyes intense on mine, she said, "Sometimes, I just get so tired o' livin'. I just want to be dun' wit' it all. No point in it wit'out me Seamus. Yer young, ye probably canno' understand."

One palsied hand lay between us on the bar. Without thinking, I slid my hand onto hers and squeezed her cold fingers.

We began to talk, sometimes the three of us, sometimes just us two. For three hours, we talked, quiet and intense, in that same way I had seen her do with Sime when I'd walked in.

People came and went from the pub, but no one took a seat at the front bar. Sime moved between rooms, reentering the conversation just when Kathleen needed him most. Sime was a man who had known and loved

Seamus Muldoon his entire life and, in this way, willingly shared a portion of the widow's burden.

Layers of sadness and sharp-edged pain were peppered with moments of laughter, and memories sprung to life in the telling. It was just after midnight, and I felt myself swimming upwards out of a deep and intimate pool of emotion. The three of us surfaced simultaneously, blinking in the figurative sunlight after hours submerged.

Seeking a lighter note on which to end the evening, Sime said, "Kat'leen, Jennifer was told 'bout a cemetery near here that contains the grave o' a famous Irishman. Do ye happen to know o' such a place an' such a grave?"

"Aye," Kathleen said. "But hold yer whist, Sime FitzPatrick. Are ye tryin' to tell me that there's somethin' in the whole o' Ireland ye dunna' know?" Kathleen's dark button eyes glittered with mischievous life and a grin transformed her grieving face.

"Aye, an' ye've caught me," Sime said, hanging his head in mock shame. "But I dunna' feel like a total gobshite. Jennifer's been askin' all o'er 'bout this supposed famous Irishman's grave, an' so far, no one has any information."

Turning her attention to me, Kathleen said, "Tis Michael Bodkin, an' he's buried in Rahoon New Cemetery. I'll take ye there tomorrow mornin', Jennifer, if ye like."

Scaling the Cemetery Wall:

A Continuation of my Time with Kathleen

Who, I hear you ask, is Michael Bodkin? Michael Bodkin, I now know, is a man for whom James Joyce penned the Irish literary figure Michael Furey from his short story *The Dead*, part of a collection entitled *The Dubliners*.

Born in 1879, Bodkin fell in love with and courted Nora Barnacle, a woman who later married James Joyce. Before he could ask for Nora's hand in marriage, Bodkin, at the age of 21, succumbed to tuberculosis. However, he left a lasting impression on Nora and she described him in detail to Joyce.

Bodkin captured Joyce's imagination and the character Michael Furey was born. Okay, so he's no William Butler Yeats or Oscar Wilde, but, as my brother Tom would say, I wouldn't kick him out of bed for eating crackers.

"So, how long ye been walkin' cemeteries?" Kathleen asked when I climbed into the passenger seat of her 1990 Honda Accord and buckled up for the bumpy, slushy ride. The weather had grown warmer over the last several days, and wetter. Rain came down in sheets throughout the hour and a half long drive. The windscreen wipers pumped back and forth against the tumult.

"Pretty much all my life," I said, staring out at the bucketing rain and scowling sky. "Kathleen, it's really nice of you to do this, but with this rain, wouldn't you rather just go have a nice breakfast somewhere than drive to a cemetery?"

"Ah, yeah, no, it'll let up afore we get there," she answered, her tone confident. "So, what came first, walkin' cemeteries er huntin' ghosts?"

"Cemeteries," I said, laughing. "My brother Jim and I used to go cemetery walking when I was a little girl and I've been hooked on it ever since."

"Cemeteries are peaceful places, dunna' ye think?"

"I do, yes, but I know not everyone feels that way. I like to read the inscriptions on the gravestones and make up

88

stories about the people's lives. It's also a great place to collect names for fictional characters."

"Ye dunna' name yer make believe people after real live dead ones, now do ye?"

"No," I said, smiling at her choice of words. "I mix and match."

"Oh, an' I see," she said, squinting into the rain rippled windscreen. "An' I suppose that's 'nuff to keep the American lawyers an' such at bay."

"Yes, I suppose it is."

"The Americans I've met o'er the years, present company excepted, a'course, all look like they're spoilin' fer a fight. Na'er have understood what it is that drives 'em on so."

"It is, unfortunately, a common trait in the U.S."

"Dunna' get me wrong," she said, still contemplating, as she took a hairpin turn at hair-raising speed. "The Irish luv to scrap an' our history is checkered wit' violent nonsense. Seamus an' me, we used to talk 'bout how we thought it might be changin' fer the better, becomin' more peaceable like, an' I think it is. Even Northern Ireland seems to be comin' 'round."

"The people I've met in Ireland have been very kind to me. You volunteering to take time out of your Saturday morning to take me to the cemetery is a real example of that. I'm sad to say that I don't think many Americans would do the same."

"Aye, an' I'd agree wit' ye. But I think that yer one o' them that would, an' that's all that counts. What do ye think o' that new president o' yers?"

"Well, I didn't vote for him. I'm a little concerned about his volatility and what I fear may be his ignorance on how a democracy is supposed to work, but I'm not very political so, unfortunately, I'm on the ignorant side myself."

"To me, this Trump character, he's the stereotype o' the worst American I've e'er run up against on Holiday in Ireland. He doesna' understand er accept any way but his own an' that's a dangerous thing. An' he luvs the power. An' the luv o' power is a dangerous thing."

We fell silent, each thinking her own thoughts about America, Ireland, or something else altogether, as we drove on along twisting, turning roads and rolling hills that, due to the pouring rain, were free of animals. We passed through spots of dense forest, every shade of green you can imagine, rollicking among rock, skinny trunked trees, shallow, bubbling brooks, and tiny waterfalls. At other points we found ourselves surrounded by barren landscapes of brown and gold, though dull on this day, with no sun to kiss their tips and bring them to ethereal life. We moved through villages crammed with colorful shops and pubs, hugged in close by cobblestone sidewalks and ancient stone walls, bell towers and church steeples towering in the background.

It was a companionable silence and I realized I enjoyed this woman's company very much. The pain I'd seen etched in her features the night before looked somehow softer this morning, despite the fact her face was a mask of fierce concentration as she pushed on through the rain toward our destination. I felt oddly giddy at the thought that she seemed to appreciate my company as well.

Sime had known, it seemed, what was needed for Kathleen, maybe for me too. He'd put us together so that we might meet those needs for each other. Sime was smart, wise, kind, insightful, and a skilled observer of the human animal; the perfect mix of ingredients for a human service professional (or a gifted bartender).

At last, Kathleen turned up a narrow, graveled two track, wound along it just long enough for me to begin to worry about getting stuck in the mud, and stopped the car in front of a pair of tall wrought iron gates. As if on cue, the rain stopped.

The sun emerged from behind a deep black cloud, and a rainbow, brilliant against the gunmetal sky, winked into view in an arch above the cemetery. Kathleen stepped out of the car and trudged, with me close on her heels, toward the imposing gates.

Standing water was everywhere. Mud and sludge clung to the bottoms of my sneakers, resulting in a disturbing slurping noise with every step I took. Behind the cemetery gates, patches of loamy green earth were visible between areas of soupy bog water.

Kathleen rattled the gate. "The bleedin' thing's locked," she said and, as if to prove her point, rattled it again.

"Have ye e'er heard o' such shite? What do they think, som'un's goin' to steal the headstones?"

The rock wall was a little less than five feet high and had plenty of jagged places to act as footholds if a person was of a mind to climb it. Had I been on my own, I likely would have turned back upon discovering the locked gate, but my new friend looked so disappointed and had driven so far to bring us to this place that I decided I needed to be up for the challenge.

"Would it be considered breaking and entering if a person were to find another way in?" I asked, watching her expression closely for a hint of what she would like me to do.

"It wouldna', no" she said, and her answer was quick, leading me to believe my assumption was correct and she really did want me to find a way to visit Michael Bodkin's grave.

"An' fer sure an' the caretaker dunna' even know it's locked. The thing probably clanged shut behind him and he na'er checked to see. Asides, who 'round here's goin' to tell on ye?" Kathleen's face was alight with a healthy excitement, as if the possibility of a little delinquency had erased decades of pain and hardship.

"All right, then," I said, eyeing the wall for the most user-friendly access point. "Keep a lookout for the Garda. I'm going to scale this thing."

She giggled like a schoolgirl and the sound bolstered me. I am not a gifted athlete and am usually timid about such physical adventures as this. But, between an ancient waiting cemetery and bringing some little bit of fun into a grieving woman's life, I was properly motivated to give it my all.

About five hundred feet beyond the gate, the wall sloped downward, following the cut of the hill, and I thought that spot might be my best bet at success. Walking toward it, I realized that the footholds in the stone were better defined and appeared nice and solid for the climb. This would work as my entry point.

Stones jutted out just above my head and I gripped them, my fingers curling around the damp, jagged surface of rock. Next, I set one sneakered toe on a rock near the base of the wall, following it with the other on the next rock up. In this way, I managed to climb the outside of the stone wall with relative ease.

Pulling myself onto the top of the wall, I sat for a moment getting my bearings, grateful for the comfortable width of ledge on which my butt was perched. Wet seeped through the seat of my blue jeans to the long underwear underneath and I shivered when a gust of wind washed through me. I had abandoned my jacket in Kathleen's car and was wearing only a sweatshirt over a long-sleeved T. There was water in the air and the wind carried a bite.

Below me, just inside the cemetery, was a long trench of mud, peat, and bog water. If I was to have any chance of missing it, I would have to jump clear of the trench onto semi-dry land. I didn't hold out a lot of hope that I could pull off this bit of simple gymnastics, but since I didn't relish being knee deep in icy muck, I had to try.

Kathleen stared up at me with a bright smile and a light in her eye. Taking a deep breath, I swung my legs over the side and searched for footholds to make my way down. One foot found a groove. The other foot found one a few inches down. One hand grabbed a triangular corner of jutting rock; the other found its twin.

So far so good. I was about a third of the way down the other side of the wall. Another few feet and I would be in position to make the backward leap.

And then it happened. My right foot, slick with watery mud, lost its grip on the toehold and slid out from beneath me. The sudden, violent tug of my body weight wrenched my fingers from the rocks above my head and I went crashing, butt first, into the boggy trench.

The impact, and the shock of icy water pouring into the waistband of my jeans, worked together to knock the breath out of me. After my initial shriek during the fall, I could produce no more sound than a brittle gasp for air.

Kathleen peered over the wall, her hand over her mouth, trying, without success, to stifle a guffaw. Once I caught my breath and realized that, other than having filled my knickers with cemetery bog, I was essentially unhurt, I started laughing too. We may never know if it was my abbreviated shriek or the gaggle of giggles that brought the grave diggers running.

The top of the graveyard where I had scaled the wall was perched on a hill. Several hundred feet in, the ground sloped downward into a valley and then rose and fell again. Thus, the two men digging the grave would have only been visible to me, or I to them, when I'd been perched on top of the wall.

Since they were busy digging and I was busy breathing and chanting the silent mantra, *I think I can; I think I can,* we'd managed to miss spotting one another. My money is on Kathleen's peel of laughter, as opposed to my brief shriek or soft thud, that alerted them to the drama unfolding at the top of the hill.

At any rate, there they were, on either side of me, gripping my arms and plucking me out of the muck. Me arse made an unpleasant suction-popping noise and I found myself standing on shaking legs, dank ooze slithering along the inner leg of my sopping jeans.

"What now, do ye think ye were doin' there, Missus?" One of the men, dressed in grimy overalls, asked, his tone incredulous.

I was saved from having to respond when Kathleen let go another peel of laughter on the other side of the wall. The men's eyes, all four of them, left my bedraggled figure to peer over the wall at my accomplice.

"Well, I'll be good god damned," the man, who'd had yet to speak, said when he saw her. "If it isna' Kat'leen Muldoon, in the flesh.

"Keegan an' I been keepin' an eye out fer ye, Missus, hopin' ye'd be by sooner than later. Yer man has a right nice spot down the hillock o'er there." Stretching an arm across the expanse of sodden ground, he pointed to the rolling hills from which they'd come a moment before.

"But ye'd be after knowin' that now, wouldna' ye, havin' been present at the lowerin'."

"An' who's this that brought ye by, then?" The first man asked, eyeing me in a way I couldn't quite read.

"I brought her, ye bleedin' eejit," Kathleen spat the words into the wind, her face a hornet's nest of irritation. "An' her backside wouldna' be co'ered in cemetery muck if ye'd checked the gate 'afore commencin' yer labors.

"Who e'er heard o' lockin' a cemetery gate?" She continued to sputter. "I finally work up the courage to visit me poor old Seamus, an' ye lock me out.

"This kind American woman wouldna' let a little thing like a locked gate stop her from makin' her way inside. I'll tell ye that much. Ye should be ashamed o' yerself, Column O'Bannion."

When the other of the two men cracked a grin at the dressing down of his colleague, Kathleen turned a spurious eye on him. "An' yer just as much to blame, Keegan O'Donnell. After me the way ye've been to come pay me respects. Badgerin' me e'ery chance ye got.

"It'll be good fer ye, Kat'leen," she mimicked in a grumbly contralto. "It'll help ye close down the grief.

"Like shite it will. What do the likes o' ye know 'bout a grievin' soul such as mine? Nuthin', that's what."

She was angry and near tears. I looked back at the two men who continued to hold lightly to my upper arms and was surprised to see them both smiling broadly in the wake of her tirade.

Extricating myself, I took a tentative step toward the wall to be closer to Kathleen. "Seamus is buried here in Rahoon?"

My voice came out so soft I wasn't sure she had heard me, but her bird-like head did that slow pivot toward the sound and she looked into my eyes. "Aye," and before she could say more, her face dissolved into anguished tears.

For the first time, Column addressed me. "Yer all right then, Missus?"

I nodded.

He left me then and hurried to the cemetery gate, tugging the giant key ring from the pocket of his coveralls as he did so. In another instant, it was unlocked and creaking open on rusty hinges.

Kathleen collapsed into his arms. He held her there, rocking slowly while the wind whipped her head scarf away from her grief ravaged features.

I felt the pressure of tears sting hot behind my eyes as I watched the tender scene unfold. The man she'd called

Keegan, gave me a nudge, producing a dirty, red checked hanky from the back pocket of his grubby pants.

Who was I, covered from the waist down in bog water and chunks of cemetery mud, to claim myself too good to accept his gentleman's offering? I took it and blew my nose.

"Grateful to ye, we are," he said as he bent toward my ear. "This is the first time since Seamus took sick that she's had any spit in her at all. She'll start comin' back to us now, an' she will. I seen it 'afore. Ye fallin' like ye did in that bit o' stinky peat was just the thing to help her through."

"She's a long way to go," I said, unconsciously mimicking the Irish-Speak to which I'd grown so accustomed.

"Aye, she's that," Keegan admitted, nodding solemnly. "But she had to get a start, an' the fact she hadna' dun that was the worry fer us all."

"But Seamus only died three weeks ago. It often takes people a lot longer than that to begin to come to grips with such a loss."

Frowning, Keegan peered down at me. "Aye, an' I know, but he's been dyin' fer five years. Wasna' supposed to live beyond a year when he got diagnosed.

"Sheer stubbornness kept him here. Pour sod didna' want to go until Kat'leen came to accept the inevitability o' it. Finally, even Seamus couldna' deny the reaper his due."

I felt sucker punched. All the talking we'd done the night before, all the reminiscing, I'd been certain Seamus's death had been sudden, or that if it had been an illness, at least it hadn't been a long, drawn out affair.

Neither Kathleen nor Sime had mentioned how Seamus had died and I hadn't asked. Had Kathleen been a client in my office, I would have done so, but this was a different scenario and I wasn't treating her; I was just being a friend.

Now, the puzzle pieces were slipping into place. Sime had seen my arrival at the pub as serendipitous and had used it to help pry Kathleen out of her deep hole of denial and despair. Once he could see she'd begun to trust me, he'd introduced my interest in finding the famous Irishman's grave.

Michael Bodkin may or may not have been the "famous" Irishman I'd been looking for, but he'd been laid to rest in the same cemetery as her cherished Seamus. Her offer to take me there, had told Sime he'd played his cards masterfully.

Kathleen Muldoon needed someone to accompany her to the graveyard but couldn't bear being at the center of the attention, as well meaning as it was. I was a compassionate stranger from America who would be leaving soon enough.

The locked gate, my fumbled attempt to scale the wall, Column and Keegan materializing out of nowhere to pluck me out of the mud, all felt like much needed comic relief and more than a little serendipity. I am grateful to whatever higher power is out there for the beauty of this moment.

I came out of my reverie to find Keegan studying me, a soft smile playing about his lips. "I can see by yer eyes, that it's all makin' a bit o' sense to ye now."

I nodded. "Yes, it is." Smiling up at him, I said, "Kathleen brought me here to see the grave of a famous Irishman,

Michael Bodkin. I've gone to all this trouble, it seems I should at least see his grave. Can you take me to it?"

The smile became a full-on grin and the grin became a hearty laugh. Keegan said, "Aye, Missus, all ye need to do is look down. In point o' fact, ye made a right fine arse print in the muck there at the edge. Yer standin' on it."

A few nights later, I visited the barkeep Sime, the orchestrator of my road trip with Kathleen. I hadn't seen Kathleen Muldoon since our time together at Rahoon Cemetery, but Sime said she'd been reconnecting with people in town. Allowing herself to laugh, cry, and reminisce with the people who loved her was putting color in her cheeks and giving her an appetite for the first time in five years.

"Sime," I asked after hearing this update. "Have you ever considered becoming a psychologist? I think you'd be a good one."

He looked at me with twinkling eyes. "Jennifer," he asked. "Have ye e'er considered becomin' a barkeep? I think ye'd be a good one."

CHAPTER 8

Encounters with Old Friends and New

3 Stories

"It's the Struggle what makes us Interestin'."

The night of Angela's mum's birthday party had arrived. Like Cinderella, I donned my most formal party clothes, blue jeans, t-shirt, cardigan, and brand new waterproof tennis shoes. Sticking my head in the sink, I scrunched it curly, applied my favorite lipstick, 99 cents from a bin at Walgreen's, and lacquered up my fingernails in robin's egg blue polish, also found in the Walgreens bin. Strapping on my fanny pack, I strolled out the door.

At five after 7:00, the pub was already packed, and I was forced to press through a sea of ruddy Irish faces to get to the bar, where I was to meet Angela and Matthew. Though Angela was nowhere in sight, I spotted Matthew at the opposite end of the bar, being manhandled by a giant ginger-haired gorilla. I'm guessing it was one of his uncles.

Matthew caught my eye and raised a glass in greeting. His uncle's massive doughy palm pounded into his back, sending liquid sloshing over the rim and Matthew careening forward into a large knot of Irish wrestlers. The men set him back on his feet and spun him in my direction, all without a pause in the conversation.

"Hi, Jennifer," Matthew said as he struggled to catch his breath. Holding tight to the lip of the bar, he managed to keep his balance among the undulating Irish. "Glad you made it."

"It was so nice of you and your aunt to include me," I said. "Where's the birthday girl?"

"See that archway over there?" He pointed in the direction of a heaving mass of checked shirts and brown corduroys clogging a doorway to the right of the main bar.

"Your Uncles?" I asked, unnecessarily.

Matthew nodded, dragging his eyes from the terrifying spectacle back to me. "Sometimes it's really hard for me to believe they all came out of her. Wait until you see her. She can't weigh more than 90 pounds."

The barkeep worked his way over to take my drink order. "What'll ye have, Missus?" He looked like the rest, massive shoulders, and a belly that could rival Santa's. The sleeves of his blue and gray checked shirt were rolled to the elbows, displaying forearms as big around as my calf, and covered in patches of orange fur against a Cream of Wheat background.

"Jamie's and Ginger," I said, without hesitation.

Matthew's young face broke into an amused grin. Remember, he was born and raised in Boston, first generation Irish American. In other words, pretty darned American. "It hasn't taken you long to acclimate to your surroundings."

I grinned back, feeling my face heat up. Being impressionable and a natural mimic, I am constantly monitoring my tendency to copy the local phrasing and inflection. Reaching into my fanny pack for money to pay the barkeep, I said, "It's kind of infectious."

"It is that," he replied, with a lilt that hadn't been there a moment before. Returning to American born Bostonian, he said, "Put your money away. It's an open bar."

I goggled at him. "An open bar!" I stared around me at the crowd, most of whom had the look of the heavy drinker. "It's going to cost somebody a feckin' fortune," I said, this time consciously allowing the Irish accent welling up inside me to push to the surface. "If ye don't mind me askin,' who's footin' the bleedin' bill?"

"Oh, God," he said, and moaned. "Now you sound just like the rest of the family. I'll have to start calling you Auntie Jennifer."

Sobering, he said, "The pub is doing the whole thing, on the house. They love my Great Gran and my Great Grandad was in here every afternoon for a pint up to two days before he died. They would do anything and everything for her."

Matthew, pride in his voice and tenderness shining in his eyes, said, "They even subsidized some of the travel costs for a few members of the family who didn't have the funds to do it on their own."

"Wow. That's incredible."

He nodded. "Good people," he said, his tone grave, measured, older than his 22 years. "Loyal."

Shifting to a lighter note, he said, "Looks like the bottleneck to see Great Gran is thinning out. Come on, I'll introduce you."

I poured my ginger into my Jamie's, made eye contact with the barkeep who winked in return, and followed Matthew through the arched doorway and into the alcove where 100-year-old Mary Margaret was holding court.

Mrs. Angus MacLeod was a diminutive woman, seated in a high-backed wooden chair at the end of a small, rectangular table. Small, hardworking hands, arthritic now and spotted with age, were folded on the table in front of her.

Her back was straight, her face elfin, the green eyes sharp. She wore her wispy white hair in a no-nonsense style, cut short and combed away from her face. Unadorned by makeup or jewelry, her pale lips curved in the barest hint of a smile, she exuded a strength of will that belied the thin shoulders and frail frame.

I felt like I was about to bow to the queen. Matthew, sensing my anxiety, gave my elbow a squeeze as he steered me forward to make the introductions.

"Hello Great Gran," he said, bending to land a light kiss on her paper-thin cheek. "I've brought Jennifer over to meet you. She's the woman Auntie Angela and I met on the bus." Walking around behind her chair, Matthew took a seat to her left and I stepped forward and offered my hand.

"Hello, Mrs. MacLeod," I said, my voice not even shaking. "I hope you are having a wonderful birthday. It was so kind of Angela and Matthew to include me in your celebration."

Mary Margaret MacLeod took my hand in a strong, dry grip. Her face illuminated into a broad smile and her eyes danced in her wrinkly face. "Sit down, Jennifer," her voice clear and young. "An' tell me all 'bout yer life."

"I'd much rather hear about yours," I said as I pulled out the chair to sit. It was hard to believe Matthew and I had her all to ourselves.

"A'course ye would, but I wouldna', ye see, havin' been there fer most o' it. Angela an' Mat'hew tell me ye practice psychology an' that yer a writer on top o' it."

"I am."

"An' that yer on 'bout writin' a book on the village. Angela says we're all goin' to be in it. Is that so?"

"Well, not exactly," I said, giving her a smile. "I'm setting a novel in Ireland and I'm here to meet people and learn more about the Irish culture and lifestyle."

"A novel," she mused. "That's a made-up story, isna' it? Na'er had much use fer make believe, but I know there's the sort who read it."

Okay, so I'd lost a few points. Before I could think what to say to try and redeem them, she spoke again. "This book o' yers, yer goin' to base it in Connemara, is that right?"

"Actually, I've spent much of my time in the southwest of Ireland, so I thought I might begin the novel there and expand outward."

She scowled, and I could feel a whole rack of points slide off my overall score. "Connemara is no' like any other part o' Ireland. Take me advice. Don't be foosterin' yer writin' down Dublin way.

"A'course, if ye want yer made up people to skip through the streets o' Ennis, ye go right ahead an' do it. I canno' stop ye. But do ye want to know what I think?"

I leaned in, eager for her wisdom.

"I think ye'll do better settin' yer book in Connemara. The well runs deeper here. Ye'll have a better book fer it, wit' better characters, more real, even if they're made up. Those feckers in Ennis havena' struggled in 200 years. The people of Connemara are still strugglin' today."

She gave my hand a pat. "It's the struggle what makes us interestin'."

We talked for another few minutes, Matthew quietly observing from the other side of the table, before others crowded in, indicating our time with the queen was drawing to a close. I told her I would take her words to heart, wished her a happy birthday, and thanked her again for allowing me to be a part of her big day.

Mary Margaret's parting words as I turned to go: "Aye, an' ye'll write the novel here in Connemara an' we'll all o' us be in it. Say ye will, Woman!"

Waiting a beat for a response I was too flustered to provide, she said, "The answer's yes, ye bleedin' eejit. It's me birthday. Ye'll give me what I want an' we'll say no more 'bout it!"

A cheer went up among the ten or twelve people now surrounding us in the room. Though they had no idea about what they were cheering, the sentiment was passionately echoed throughout the rest of the bar.

"An' it's dun," Mary Margaret said. Had she a gavel, I believe she would have pounded it on the table. "Ye'll get yer wee bottom into gear an' write me a make-believe story wit' all these grand folk fittin' inside, every one wit' a starrin' role. An' ye'll have it to me by this day year next, in time fer me hundred an' first birthday. I'll be expectin' it."

Matthew and I found his aunt and she took me around, introducing me to her nine brothers. They were in clusters of twos and threes, so it didn't take as long as you might imagine. Her sisters were a little harder to track down and, once tracked, were a little harder to get away from, but it was great fun meeting them all.

Angus and Mary Margaret's brood is close knit and colorful, and utterly overwhelming. There were moments when it seemed the laughing, Guinness swilling, bear-hugging, storytelling Irish were coming at me from all sides.

Fortunately, Matthew, a sensitive soul empathically tuned to my walls-closing-in sensation, three times pulled me from the fray to step outside for a breath of air. Turns out he's had plenty of practice. His partner Kevin, who steadfastly refused to join him on this excursion, frequently displays similar symptoms when in the presence of the O'Shea-MacLeod's.

Brendan the Friendly Firefighter

The pub where Mary Margaret's party was being held was built in the middle 1700's and is broken up into a number of separate cozy rooms, each one outfitted with its own small bar and peat burning fireplace. Little round tables, surrounded by low cushioned stools and booths tucked away in curtained alcoves, completed the old-fashioned dollhouse atmosphere of the place. Somewhere around 10:45, I sought refuge in the smallest of the little rooms where, remarkably, the barkeep, a young guy named Uri who'd arrived from Poland less than a month before, was the only inhabitant.

I sat at the bar and ordered a shot of Powers, straight, no ice, Big Jesus's contribution to my Irish alcoholic learning curve.

Side Note: *The first time I ordered Jameson and Ginger from Big Jesus, he made such a face that I thought he might be ill. "An' I suppose they taught ye that one down Cork way, the miserable lightweight fuckers."*

Tugging his big hand down his world-weary face, Big Jesus offered up a long-suffering sigh. "Well, yer under my wing now, whether either o' us likes it er not."

Plunking the shot of Powers on the bar before me, he said, "Now, it's a sipper, an' smooth as silk. Yer tutelage has begun. All I can say is, thank God, Woman, I'm no' too late."

Okay, back to Tuesday night's party: After three hours of constant verbal stimulation, it was a nice break to find myself in a quiet spot with a person who barely spoke English. Uri and I sat in companionable silence for a number of delicious minutes before being discovered.

At first, it didn't seem as calamitous as either Uri or I had feared. The man was alone and, while he was happily grinning away when he hopped onto the bar stool next to me, he wasn't wrapping a massive arm around my shoulder and breathing beer in my face. Nor was he bursting forth with verse 1 of 4000 in an offkey rendition of some horrifying Irish drinking song, all the while swaying to and fro with such enthusiasm that it sent the room spinning and the floor rising to meet me.

"Hiya," he said, extending his hand. "The name's Brendan, an' yers?"

Smiling, I gave him my name and shook his hand. Okay, I felt a little uncomfortable when he held onto my hand a few seconds longer than seemed appropriate, but I'd been so battered and bruised by Angela's good-natured brothers and sisters that I shrugged it off easily enough.

"Are you related to Mary Margaret?" I asked and took a sip of my Powers.

"No, just a friend o' the family. Hard not to be when ye've lived in the village all yer life." He gave the sleeve of my cardigan a little tug. "Now, what's yer story, Jennifer? I've noticed ye 'round town the last few days, but somehow, I canno' see ye being a part o' this clan. Yer too wee. I grew up wit' the MacLeod's. Even the girls had outgrown ye by the time they hit the age o' seven."

I laughed. "No, I'm not a member of the family. Angela and I met on the bus and she was nice enough to invite me."

"So, yer on Holiday. Aye, that's good. It's nice an' quiet here this time o' year."

118

There was an explosion of laughter from another room. We looked at each other and laughed. "Well," he added, "Generally speakin' anyway."

Brendan works with the Fire Service. He talked to me about his two grown children, his recent divorce, and the death of his mother. I felt a little like I was back in my office, but that was okay.

The sensation of being back at work was particularly striking when Brendan began to describe some of his experiences on the job. It didn't take long to recognize the signs of unresolved Posttraumatic Stress Disorder, secondary, a common enough affliction of first responders. His drinking had slowed down, and a few nervous ticks were making their way to the surface as he related nightmarish details he'd encountered when responding to motor vehicle accidents.

Once begun, the stories kept coming, one after another, for over the next two hours. Again and again, tears welled in his eyes. He'd wipe them away with the back of a meaty hand and keep on going. An hour into his monologue, I felt ready to put my head down on the bar and go to sleep but couldn't find a sensitive way to extricate myself.

At last, the stories stopped, and Brendan appeared to come out of his trance. "Oh, Jennifer," he said, looking up at the clock on the wall behind the bar. "I didna' mean to let it get so late. Just me blatherin' on, an' ye bein' kind 'nuff to listen."

I smiled and assured him that the conversation had been a good one and I appreciated his taking the time to talk to me. I could hear the party at last winding down in the main bar.

I slid off the stool. "It was really nice meeting you, Brendan. I'm going to find Angela and say goodnight."

"I'd be happy to walk ye home, make sure ye get there, safe like."

"That's nice of you, but I'll be fine," and I walked out in search of Angela and Matthew.

At that time, I really wasn't too concerned about Brendan's offer to walk me home, though I definitely knew better than to take him or anyone else up on it. And he didn't press the matter, so it soon left my mind.

Onward to Dingle

I met up with my friend Dawn, who'd flown into Cork three days before, and we headed to the Dingle Peninsula. Once in the rental car, Dawn programmed the GPS. An Irish woman's pleasant voice informed us that the trip to Dingle would take a little over two and a half hours...

The bitch lies.

Okay, so we did stop for coffee, lunch, dessert, and shopping in the little villages along the way, but still...

The bitch lies.

Narrow twisting roads, encased on either side by ancient stone walls, wound through picturesque villages and mountainous countryside. It was a lovely drive, but slow going, and much of the time we weren't sure we were headed in the right direction. Have I mentioned that the bitch lies?

At times, the bitch stopped talking altogether, leaving us to wonder if the mountain pass, both steep and skinny, was taking us anywhere other than the edge of a cliff.

Three hours passed. Road signs announced, in Gaelic and English, the names of upcoming villages, but not a word about Dingle.

Four hours passed. The tiny hybrid rental car continued to climb. Our ears popped.

Swirling mists blanketed the tops of the mountains. We continued to ascend.

By now it was 4:30 in the afternoon. Dusk was unfolding all around us. Still no sign (literally) of Dingle. Our ears popped some more. The lying bitch was silent.

At last, we saw a sign for Dingle and an arrow pointing straight ahead. The bitch, finally deciding to break her silence, told us to turn right. Dawn looked at me. I looked at Dawn. We followed the arrow...which took us to Conor Pass.

Conor Pass is a narrow, winding road that makes the other narrow winding roads we'd traveled that day look wide. If we met a car coming from the opposite direction, we would have to stop, hug the hillside, and wait for it to pass.

And, while you're conjuring an image of the ancient, anorexic road whose surface was pock marked by divots and lumped with cancerous tumors, consider replacing the word *winding* with the phrase *hairpin turn*. Now, add sheep. All I can say is, it's a good thing Dawn was a race car driver in a past life.

At long last, we arrived in Dingle; it was after 7:00 p.m. We'd left Cork at 10:30 that morning.

The bitch lies.

Dawn parked the car in the hotel lot, and we went in search of medicinal strength beverages. We found them.

It was a fun evening of great food and friendly people. We even stumbled onto a combination bar and hardware store.

The following morning, we made our way back to my cottage in the Connemara fishing village, a drive the GPS informed us would take about four hours.

124

Seven hours later, night had fallen, and we were still driving.

The bitch lies.

CHAPTER 9

A New Friend Who Wasn't and Unsung Heroes

5 Stories

Brendan, the Too-Friendly Firefighter

(Not a funny story)

In this story, you will meet Colleen and Joe. For their kindness and quick thinking, I will always be grateful. Rory and Big Jesus you will recall from the earlier section on barkeeps.

It was a fish and chips night for me, along with a glass of white wine. Having said goodbye to my friend Dawn earlier that day, I sat alone at a corner table reading my Kindle by the light of my iPhone flashlight. I was thus

126

engrossed when someone pulled a chair up to my table and sat down next to me. I looked up to see Brendan, the man with the fire service I had met at Angela's mum's birthday party a couple of weeks before.

"Hello, Jennifer," he said, squeezing in until our knees were touching under the table. "Do ye mind if I keep ye company fer a while? I need to grab a bit o' dinner an' I hate to eat alone."

"Sure," I said and could hear the hesitation in my voice. He was right on top of me and it was anything but comfortable. Brendan is a large man and I felt squished into the corner. "But I think you and I would both be more comfortable with a little breathing room. Why don't you sit across from me, so it's easier to talk?"

His mouth curved into a smile that failed to meet his eyes. "I think we'll be grand talkin' just like this," he said, making no attempt to pull back. "Ye have a soft voice; it'll be easier fer me to hear ye if I sit in close."

A shiver passed through me. He seemed a different man from the one I'd met the time before, and I didn't like the transformation.

Looking over Brendan's shoulder, I noticed one patron, Joe, a nice guy I'd met on a few occasions, watching us intently. The server, Colleen, was also alert to what felt to me like a rapidly devolving "situation". It helped to make eye contact with these kind people and to know I wasn't on my own.

Colleen nodded and came over to my table. "I'll just put this in a box fer ye, Jennifer. Would ye like to pay now as well?"

"Yes, thanks so much," I said and Colleen and I both understood we were working together to get me out of there.

"It's 14 euros an' I'll wait an' take it fer ye."

"No, Colleen," Brendan said, waving her away. "Put Jennifer's supper on me tab. I'll settle up afore we go."

"That's nice of you," I said. "But not necessary. I really do have to be going."

He didn't budge. Colleen held her ground and I could see Joe abandoning his seat at the bar to come walking toward us. As Joe came to stand behind Colleen, she left to get the box for my fish. The two seemed to be protecting me; I didn't believe I was imagining it.

Joe is a man of few words. Standing there at the table where Brendan continued to pen me in, he said nothing. Nor was he smiling as he stared down at the man who was easily twice his size.

Colleen brought me my fish, handing it to Joe. "Now, there ye are, Jennifer, and yer bill's sorted as well. We want to buy yer meal fer tonight as a welcome to our village." She gave me a wink.

"And I've got yer fish fer ye," Joe said, speaking to me, but looking at Brendan. "All that's left is fer ye to make yer way to the door."

At last, Brendan pushed his chair back to let me out. Handing me my fish, Joe stepped in front of Brendan, effectively separating me from the larger man. I knew now, beyond a shadow, that Joe and Colleen were watching out for me.

"Thanks so much, Joe," I said. "I appreciate it." I slipped out the front door and hurried down the street toward my apartment.

I hadn't made it two blocks before Brendan materialized from a side street and fell into step beside me. "I wouldna' be much o' a gentleman if I didna' walk ye back to yer place., now would I?"

"That's nice of you," I said, "But I make it a rule not to let anyone walk me home."

"Rules," he said. "Were made to be broken."

I have been lucky in my life. Until this moment, I have never felt threatened as I did this night on the nearly empty village street. I said, "Well, I'm not breaking this one," and picked up my pace to put distance between us.

In less than a second, he was beside me again. I didn't know what to do, but I knew I couldn't risk walking toward the apartment.

We'd come to the door of Rory's bar. "Goodbye." Tossing the word over my shoulder, I pulled open the pub door and went inside.

Brendan followed me in and took the bar stool next to me. Behind the bar, Rory's eyes met mine and he raised a brow. I held his gaze and then turned to Brendan. "I

130

would prefer to be on my own right now, Brendan," I said. "Thanks anyway."

"No bother," he said, purposely misunderstanding. "I've nowhere else to be. I'll just keep ye company fer a bit afore I walk ye home."

To Rory, he said, "Hiya Rory. Pint o' Guinness fer me an' the lady'll have a shot o' Powers. Put 'em both on me tab."

"No," I said quickly. "I don't want you to buy me a drink and I need you to respect my wishes to have this time to myself."

"Oh, no bother," he said again and nodded to Rory, who stood frozen in place on the other side of the bar.

Rory intervened. "Brendan, the lady was right plain 'bout her preferences. I think ye'd better clear off now."

Brendan stared at him, making no move to leave.

"I guess I'll go then," I said. "Don't follow me, Brendan. Whatever it is you want; you're not going to get it from me."

To this, Brendan said nothing.

Rory's eyes slid to mine, and he gave a single, nearly imperceptible, shake of his head. Then he poured me a whiskey and pulled Brendan's Guinness, plunking it down in front of him on the bar.

Following Rory's lead, I stayed put on the barstool. The last thing I wanted to do was walk back out onto the empty sidewalk with Brendan on my heels.

We sat this way for the better part of an hour, me sipping at the Powers, but not really drinking it, Brendan putting away three pints in rapid succession. "Now then," he said, when he'd finished his third. "I'll just head to the loo an' then I'll walk ye to yer place."

As soon as the door to the men's room closed behind him, Rory came out from behind the bar, ushered me through the kitchen and out the back door. "Go on now, Jennifer. We'll keep him here 'til yer safe home."

I thanked him and did as I was told, my heart hammering against the wall of my chest like a bird trapped in a shoebox. Letting myself inside the apartment, I locked the door behind me and pulled the drapes.

132

No sooner had I settled onto the couch when my phone rang. It was the woman who'd rented me the apartment. Rory had called her the moment I left the bar. She was wonderful and, as she lives right next door, offered to come spend the night, so I would feel safe.

I thanked her, but said I thought I would be fine. She assured me that her husband would make certain Brendan didn't bother me again. It felt good to know this community of people had my back.

I was touched and grateful for the people who saw the problem and were quick to intervene on my behalf. It was, however, disturbing to see how smoothly the intervention played out. It makes me wonder just how much practice the barkeeps and wait staff have had in its execution.

A Come to Jesus Meeting, Presided over by none other than Big Jesus Himself

When I ventured into my favorite fishermen's pub for my usual 1:00 p.m. eavesdropping session, I learned from barkeep Dermot (AKA Big Jesus) that Rory, after packing Brendan off home in a cab, had made the rounds of the pubs to alert them of the situation in case it happened again.

According to Big Jesus, Joe was kicking himself for letting Brendan give him the slip. Apparently, after he and Colleen had sent me on my way, Brendan had made a pretext of heading to the bathroom, but instead, left through the pub's back door to intercept me on the street.

"Most o' us are decent 'nuff." Dermot said, pulling up a stool behind the bar so he could sit across from me. His eyes today, as they looked into mine, were dead serious. "We dunna' bully a woman into bed.

"But there's a few, like Brendan last night, used to gettin' what they want, an' doin' what it takes to get it."

He sat back, studying my face. His big hand that had been palm down on the surface of the bar, curled into a tight fist and a sharp, quick anger came into his eyes. I wouldn't want to be on the wrong side of Big Jesus the way Brendan now was.

"Thanks, Dermot," I said. I wanted to take a sip of my coffee, but I knew my hands weren't steady enough to lift the cup to my mouth. "Joe and Colleen and Rory were great last night. I'll never forget what they did for me."

The lump in my throat made it hard to get the words out. My eyes were stinging. I blinked rapidly to keep the tears from falling.

"Aw, fuck," he said, pulling a big hand down his long face, in a gesture I'd come to recognize. "I dunna' want to be scarin' ye. Yer on Holiday an' ye need to be havin' fun an' no' havin' to worry 'bout the likes o' that gobshite." Adding quickly, "An' ye won't. We'll see to that."

Recovering enough to find my voice, I said, "I've been taking a lot of long walks during the daytime. Is that not safe?"

"Ah, no, yeah, no, yer safe 'nuff in the daytime. Predators like Brendan only come out at night when they're drinkin'."

I went to take a sip of my now cold coffee, but Dermot whisked the cup away and replaced it with a fresh one. "Ye came here expectin' someplace mild, but this place ain't mild. This is wild Connemara, the wild west o' Ireland.

"Dunna' get me wrong now, I'm sure the southwest has their share o' bad blokes, but still they're tamer. An' to every one person ye have watchin' out fer ye here, ye'd have five mindin' yer house there."

Big Jesus took a long pause as he watched me drink my coffee. The three old men a few stools away from us listened in, appearing satisfied with what they'd heard. At last, he said, "I'm so sorry 'bout this, Jennifer. It's my fault ye got the wits scared out o' ye."

Incredulous, I asked, "How can that be your fault?"

136

"I was the first barkeep ye met here in Connemara. I shoulda' warned ye. Shite, ye were after tellin' me straight away that ye'd na'er been this far west 'afore. I shoulda' minded ye more."

I tried again to protest, but he waved away my words, an expression of misery etched into his features. "I'll be mindin' ye now, an' that's a promise." Setting the stool aside, indicating the come-to-Jesus-meeting was at an end, Dermot busied himself spraying hot water over a rack of glasses.

And that was the last we spoke of the incident with Brendan.

A Night Out with Big Jesus

Due to its extremely personal nature, this is a story I nearly didn't include. I decided to do so for a couple of reasons. First, I believe this to be an excellent representation of both the strength and the tenderness of the Irish culture. Second, it illustrates the character and the resilience of this good man.

Dermot (AKA Big Jesus) surprised me by asking if I'd be willing to go for a drink with him after the soccer game in which he was playing at 8:00 p.m. It would be nearly 10:00 by the time he finished the game, showered, and made it back to the bar, if that didn't feel too late? It was my last night in the village and he wanted to treat me.

Big Jesus is an interesting man, with many facets to his personality. Beneath the jokester, lurks a nature that is sensitive and introspective. An avid reader, Dermot has an astute insight into human nature, as well as a working understanding of political climates around the globe. He is also a shepherd, giving an old man a lift to his house after he's had too many pints, something I'd witnessed on more than one occasion. The longer I observed this man and his interaction with the village and its people, the more I understood the Big Jesus moniker was about more than just his hair. I wondered what in the world he wanted to talk about.

At 9:45, I made my way to meet Big Jesus. We wandered down to another pub, a place I'd only been in a handful of times over the course of the month. There, I met some colorful characters, friends of Big Jesus, I'd not met before.

Dougal, a young barkeep with sleepy blue eyes, big ears, and a lazy grin, was behind the bar. Funny and friendly, Dougal had mentored under Big Jesus for the better part of the past two years, and the hero worship was evident in the way his gaze followed the older man from doorway to barstool.

Donal and James sat opposite Dougal at the bar. These men were older, probably in their early to mid-seventies and the affection Dermot felt for them was written in the soft upward turn of his lips and the warm sparkle in his hazel eyes.

The three were engaged in playful banter when Dermot and I arrived, and they pulled him into the mix without a single break in stride. One pint and one Jamie's and Ginger later, Dermot gripped my elbow and we made our way from the bar to a quiet table near the back. Time for the talk.

"When ye first sat up at me bar almost a month ago, I fell in luv wit' yer head." This was his opener. I waited to see what would come next.

"Ye know, yer smarts," he added, poking himself in the forehead with a blunt-tipped forefinger. "It was easy to tell ye'd had education behind ye an' the wisdom to know how to use it. It didna' surprise me to learn ye were a psychologist.

"Now, the writer part surprised me. Ye dunna' look like a writer, an' I'd take that as a compliment if I was ye. Ye smile too much to be a writer. Until I met ye, I didna' know a person could put words to paper wit'out wearin' a long face to do it.

"So, anyway, like I said, I fell in luv wit' yer head. Now, yer friend Dawn, wit' her it was different. I fell in luv wit' her sweet smile. The sweetest smile I e'er seen. An' her titties. I fell in luv wit' those too, but main it was her smile."

"I think she's quite fond of you too," I said, grinning at him.

But he just shook his head and stared down into his fresh pint of Carlsberg. "No, an' I canno' go after yer friend. Ye see, I've a girlfriend, but the feelin' I had did shake me some."

"You love your girlfriend." I offered this as a statement.

He nodded and bowed his big shaggy head low over his pint. "God help me, an' I do. Fuck, it's awful. She's all fucked up wit' drugs, prescription pills like. Fuck, she's the one what gave me the scar on me arm!"

"Maybe you should consider stepping away from her."

He lifted his eyes to me and in the dim light of the bar his face was a mask of misery. "Woman, didna' ye just hear me tell ye I luv her?"

He took a long swallow of his pint, set the glass down and leaned his forearms on the table. "Fuck, I'm no prize meself, no easy bit fer her to deal wit'."

"Have you tried talking to her? Have you told her that you're worried about the drugs?"

The eyebrows went up and he gave me an incredulous stare. "Do I need to show ye the scar again?"

"It's not likely to change if you don't talk to her."

"It's not likely to change if I do." In an abrupt move, he pushed back from the table, pulled his hand down his long face. "Bah, a'course I tried to talk to her. She wouldna' listen."

"I'm sorry, Dermot," I said. I felt sad for this sweet, funny, tortured man, but wasn't sure what he was expecting of me or what I ought do next.

We sat in silence for what felt like many minutes, but was probably no more than ninety seconds or so. At last, he said, "Ah, dunna' mind me. I've had a rough couple o' months, that's all. We buried me ma an' me sister Maureen in December. It was the cancer."

"Oh no, Dermot, I'm so sorry." I wanted to reach out but wasn't certain how he'd accept it. Putting my hand over his, I squeezed briefly and then let my hand rest on the table near his.

With the knuckles of his left hand, he wiped the wet from his eyes. "Me ma, she was old, ye know? It was time. I'm the youngest at 45. Maureen was the oldest. Almost 20 years older than me. Too young to be taken by the cancer though."

"You miss her."

"Fuck, an' I miss her." His voice broke. He clenched his fist, pulled himself back from the brink.

"Tell me about her. What was she like?"

He looked at me long and steady. "Ye really want to know?"

I nodded.

"She was hard. But she was good, ye know? Her luv was hard earned, but it made ye want it all the more fer how hard it was to get it.

"I remember one time, I wasna' no more than thirteen. The first time I smoked weed. I got so pissed I couldna' see straight an' one o' me friends gave me some weed an' I smoked it.

"I got this idea in me head to climb out o' the four-story window o' our house just to get Maureen's attention. She was ignorin' me, disgusted wit' how rat arsed I was.

"I dunno' what I was thinkin', maybe that I could fly er some such shite. I woulda' fallen, but me belt loop got caught on a nail that was stickin' out o' the window ledge, an' I was just hangin' there by the loop in me pants.

"Me other brothers an' sisters were scramblin' to bring me back in through the window, but no' Maureen. Maureen wouldna' have nuthin' to do wit' it. 'Let him fall, the fucker,' she said, an' she meant it too. But that didna' mean she didna' love me. It meant that she did. Ye know what I'm sayin'?"

I smiled at him and nodded, squeezing the big hand that lay motionless on the tabletop. He squeezed back, knocked back the rest of his pint, and knuckled away the moisture that had collected in his eyes. "Appreciate yer listenin'. I dunno' what made me want to tell ye 'bout Maureen. I just did."

"I'm glad you told me about Maureen," I said. "She's worth talking about."

He offered me a sheepish grin. "I'll bet I'm the first client what's paid ye in whiskey."

I grinned back at him. "And I'll bet I'm your first customer that's paid you by listening."

Leaning in, Big Jesus gave me a kiss on the cheek. "An' ye'd be right."

Help with My Bags...Almost

I was wide awake at five the next morning, which was surprising, since I hadn't made it back to the apartment until after one. Today was the day I would say goodbye to this sleepy little fishing village and board the 7:15 a.m. bus to Shannon.

By six, I was showered, dressed, packed, and ready to head out the door. Unfortunately, there was no place open to go. The only breakfast cafe didn't open until 8:00.

I worked on my journal until 6:45 and then decided to drag my 50-pound suitcase up the several flights of steep stone steps. The prospect was daunting, and I was growing more anxious by the minute that I might not be able to do it.

Relieved to report, the bag and all its contents were successfully delivered to street level by 6:55 a.m. I was back in the apartment and collapsed on the couch catching my breath when there was a knock on my patio door.

I looked up to see three hulking figures, one more hulking than the others, standing outside. In Ireland, this time of year, daylight doesn't peek over the horizon until after 8:00 a.m. so darkness, along with the fog and mist rolling in off the sea, shrouded the identities of the men framed in the glass door.

I flipped on the outdoor light. Illuminated therein was Big Jesus himself, Sime, and Joe.

Opening the door, I said, "What sweethearts you guys are! You came to see me off?"

"What the fuck's the matter with ye, Woman?" Big Jesus said, clearly disgusted.

"We dragged our sorry arses out o' bed to do ye a good turn an' ye went an' fucked it up. Ye just may be the hardest woman to do a favor fer that I've e'er come across."

Big Jesus, running out of breath in his rant, paused to suck in air and Sime stepped in to explain. "Dermot called me an' Joe last night, askin' if we'd be willin' to come wit' him to take yer bag up the steps this mornin'. He wanted to surprise ye."

"An' wha' do we get fer our trouble?" Big Jesus wanted to know. "The bleedin' bag's already up there. The bus doesna' even come fer another 15 minutes!"

"Oh my gosh," I said, feeling the threat of tears starting behind my eyes. "That is so sweet of you guys. I was nervous that I might not be able to get the bag up the stairs, so I did it early just to get it over with."

"I hate to be breakin' the news to ye, but yer no' a normal woman." Big Jesus was pacing on the patio. Joe was mute, but grinning wide. Sime, looking like the Professor from Gilligan's Island, stood by, his pleasant features taking on an expression of analytical interest.

Big Jesus continued. "I thought when ye made fun at me bar 'bout how yer friend was always gettin' her bag toted on an' off the bus by the bus driver er some other bloke, that ye were droppin' the hint fer me to do the same fer ye. I only brought these two, so's no' to scare ye na'er to death by showin' up by meself at yer back door. But ye wasna' hintin' at all now, was ye?"

I shook my head. "No, but I really do appreciate you going out of your way to show up like this, all of you."

Sime gave a little bow. "Well, since we're here, we might as well accompany ye to the bus stop, but we'd best be leavin' now, as it'll be there in less than ten minutes time."

I grabbed my coat. Big Jesus attempted to strap my backpack over his own massive frame, failed, and instead, slung it over one shoulder. Joe carried my computer bag and Sime offered me his arm. In this way, the four of us walked up the steps and down the empty street to the bus stop. In the company of these kind-hearted men, I felt a little like Dorothy, sans Toto, from the Wizard of Oz.

I boarded the bus and stared out the window at my new friends. They stood in a row on the sidewalk, the three of them, the lion, the tin man, and the scarecrow, I'll let you decide for yourself which was which, waving and growing smaller as the bus trundled along the narrow street and out of town. Big Jesus raised a hand to his face and I wondered if he might be knuckling away a tear; I certainly knew I was.

Leaving My Suitcase on the Bus in Limerick

The bus arrived in Galway at 9:00 a.m. and I straggled off, along with the dozen or so other passengers, most of whom were commuting to work. I waited on the sidewalk for the jaws to open along the underbelly of the mechanical beast, so I could retrieve my monstrous suitcase.

The City Link bus to Limerick wouldn't arrive until half eleven, but from perusing the bus schedules online, I'd discovered I could catch a 9:30 bus to Limerick by switching to Bus Eireann. So, with the weight of two bags on my back and dragging the giant red suitcase with the wonky wheel behind me, I hotfooted it down the busy Galway street, taking a sharp left down a bumpy brick alleyway, rounding the bend to approach the Bus Eireann Station from the rear. Fifteen minutes to spare! I was exhilarated.

The bus ride to Limerick took just over three and a half hours. I parceled my time between sleep, reading, and gazing out the window. The haunted Connemara landscape gave way to mossy banks shepherding streams of rushing water that bubbled over shining, jagged rock. Brilliant green hills were dotted with sheep. After a time, these too faded into the distance, replaced by a bustling city of red, yellow, and blue storefronts. Limerick.

The bus from Galway was scheduled to arrive at the Limerick bus station at 12:30. My connecting bus was due to pull in at 12:45. This gave me 15 minutes to clamber off, snag my suitcase from the undercarriage, and make my way down the long line of busses.

Unlike the nearly empty bus that had taken me to Galway, the bus that carried me to Limerick had been filled to capacity, thus taking a good deal longer for me to disembark. By the time I stepped off onto the pavement, it was 12:42. If I wanted to catch my ride before it left the station, I would have to run.

I ran, making it to the welcoming open door of the bus to Shannon in a breathless three minutes. Wow, I thought, look at me racing around, maneuvering the public transportation system! I rock!

It was only as I placed the toe of my purple tennis shoe onto the first step of the Shannon bus, that I realized something was missing. The familiar weight of my backpack and computer bag rested between my shoulder blades, yet I had the nagging feeling that this had somehow been a little too easy.

What was it, I asked myself as I chewed my lower lip. And then, in a lightning bolt of awareness, I knew. My 50-pound suitcase was on the bus I'd just left, and embarking, right about now, on an adventure of its own. Heaven only knew when and where me and my belongings would be reunited.

Staring up at the driver, wide-eyed, I removed the toe of my shoe from the step, whirled, and ran, heart pounding, to the terminal doors and inside the bustling station. Reaching the counter, behind which stood a pleasant appearing woman with iron gray hair and silver framed cat's eye glasses, I laid my trembling hands flat on its surface and tried to pull air into my panicked lungs. Behind the glasses were the twinkling blue eyes that are the trademark of the Irish. I fought to catch my breath and slow my racing heart.

152

"My bag," I said, between gasps for air. "I left my suitcase on the bus from Galway. Has it left? Can you tell me what to do to get it back?"

Looking at me, her eyes kind, but with a sparkle of wry amusement, she said, "Oh, that bus'll be long gone, it will. Ye'll na'er catch it now." These devastating words were delivered in a cheerful tone, the common Irish inflection used when referencing lost causes and all things tragic.

Before I could respond, she went on. "Ye'll have to chase it wit' another to see if ye can catch it up. That bus what has yer luggage will be goin' back up Kilorglin way, it will. An' the next 'un to take ye there doesna' come 'til half fifteen. Ye'll na'er catch it. Ye might as well go to the end o' the line an' wait fer it to come in to nest at half twenty this evenin'."

"Um, where," I said, interrupting myself to clear my throat that was suddenly thick with mucousy dread. "Where will it go to nest?"

"Ah, that bus does a loop, it does, windin' up in Tralee at the end o' its shift."

My heart sank. Thanks to Dawn's fearless tackling of the Irish roads, I was familiar with the location of which the woman spoke. And, as Big Jesus would say, Tralee was way the fuck up by the Dingle Peninsula. I would have to get a room there and probably need to change busses at least twice for the five plus hour ride back to Shannon in the morning.

"Ah, now, it'll be grand, it will," the woman with the silver spectacles framing the twinkly blue eyes said as she took in my crestfallen countenance. "The world is round, after all."

At that moment, she turned to peer out the window at her back. "Well, Janie Mack, will ye look at that!"

Pointing, she said, "That's gas it is, absolute gas (I later learned this was a way of saying great good luck). The driver must o' stopped to chat er go to the toilet, 'cause there's the bus wit' yer bag waitin' to pull out.

"Best run an' catch it up afore it rolls away. Ye might turn things right yet."

I ran. Out the bus station door. Clattered down the steep metal steps. My feet hit the pavement, jarring my teeth

154

together, bouncing my backpack hard against my shoulder blades. I barely noticed. A full out sprint and I was waving down the bus just as it poked its big red and white nose out into the street.

The driver saw me and put on the brake. The bi-fold doors opened with a creak. "Yer lookin' fer yer bag then, Missus?" He asked from his perch high above my inconsequential little self.

Unable to catch my breath, I nodded mutely in reply.

"I watched ye get off the bus, an' I knew ye'd forgotten it. I remembered as I'd watched yer wee self wrestlin' wit' the massive thing when ye boarded in Galway. Had an attack o' conscience, ye might say. Almost gave in an' helped ye wit' it meself, I did. But it wouldna' do.

"It'd be settin' a precedent like if I was to help ye wit' yer bag. Then everybody an' his brother would be expectin' me to do it fer them as well, an' we canno' be havin' that now, can we?

"Anyway," he said, dismissing the extraneous details with a wave of his hand. "When I saw ye leave wit'out it, I pulled it off the bus meself. But when I went to find ye, ye'd disappeared into the crowd. Due to yer wee size, ye do that better than most, so I put it up in the lost luggage shed o'er to the left o' the station there.

"Ye can retrieve it from there an' ye'll be grand altogether." He pointed, and I cranked my head around, pinning my eyes on a squat red brick building a few yards away from the far end of the terminal.

The smile I felt expanding my features threatened to slip outside the bounds of my face. He tossed me one back, throwing in a wink, for good measure, and I was off to the shed, running hard, barely able to contain my joy.

Pushing open the gray metal door, the smell of damp assaulted me. One tiny filthy window near the ceiling was all the illumination the little storage room offered, but it was enough.

Squinting into the murk, I made out my battered red suitcase. It stood upright by the back wall, alone in the small square space. We embraced and, together, ventured out into the overcast Irish sky.

Of course, I knew I had missed the 12:45 bus to Shannon and would have to wait until the next one arrived at 2:30.

That was okay, I decided. I'd get into Shannon about three hours later than I'd originally planned, but it beat the heck out of tacking on another seven hours of bus travel and losing an entire day before my flight out the next.

On my way back to the main building, I glanced toward the row of busses. And could hardly believe my eyes. The bus to Shannon, the one that was to have left the station nearly 15 minutes before, was still idling in its slot.

With what was surely the one sprint left in my shaking legs, I set out across the massive parking lot at warp speed, arriving just in time to see the big mechanical jaws of the bus's undercarriage yawn open, hungry for my suitcase. I fed the beast and raced to the open door of the bus and onto the steps.

Above me, on his busly throne, sat the driver. Our eyes locked. His were squinchy, sunbursts of deep wrinkles spreading outward from the corners toward the sides of his head. In their emerald depths I saw, both compassion and triumph, the ever-present humor and weary acceptance of the human condition. Those eyes had been the first to witness the thump of shock in my own several minutes before when I'd realized that I'd left my bag on the other bus.

On the second step, I paused to catch my breath. "I can't believe you're still here," I wheezed, grateful and incredulous.

"Dunna' ye think we could all see just what was goin' on?" His tone was conversational. He wasn't looking for a response. "It was plain as the nose on yer face to all o' us when ye turned an' bolted fer the station, that ye'd left yer bag on the other bus.

"I tried to call Maxim there, the driver o' 51, but I couldna' get through. Must a'been talkin' to his wife. Married these 35 years an' still can't seem to get enough o' one another.

"Anyway, we discussed it," he said, motioning to the other passengers. "An' we decided to wait fer ye. Ye'd had enough o' a blow as it was, we decided. An' what's a few minutes wait? Nuthin' more than a bit o' spare change, that's what."

I looked from him to the sea of Irish faces on the crowded city bus and back again. Tears threatened to spill down my face and probably some snot along with them (I can be a bit snotty when emotional).

"So, what ye waitin' fer? Climb on board."

I did as I was told, pausing at the front of the bus as the kind, green-eyed driver registered my ticket. Every face on the bus was smiling. The ear-to-ear grins of a hundred or so passengers were like a taste of Heaven itself. Maybe, I thought, this was what would be waiting for all of us when we cross over into the afterlife, a public bus filled with welcoming faces. I hoped so.

The driver handed me my ticket and the busload of smiling people broke out in a round of whistles and applause. Their faces swam like an impressionist painting as the tears bubbled out over my lower lashes. My face was beginning to hurt from my own wide grin. Swiping at my tear stained cheeks, I took a little bow.

The mad applause went madder still. Raising his voice to be heard over the din, the bus driver said, "Now, sit down, Woman. We're goin' to be late!"

The man in the window seat just behind the driver motioned to the one open seat beside him, the one they'd saved for me and, with gratitude, I took it.

How truly apt it was to end my trip on this note, with the friendliness and generosity of the Irish that I'd come to know, and which plays such a big part in the magic of the Emerald Isle.

CHAPTER 10

Tidbits:
The Colorful Language
of the Irish

I n this second village I found myself doing a lot more eavesdropping than I did in the first, most of it by accident. Some of what I heard I couldn't resist reproducing here.

Smatterings of Conversations Overheard

"Oh, an' I thought I would 'bout die o' the heat!" The temperature topped out at 52 degrees Fahrenheit and was spitting rain.

"How ye keepin'?" asked a robust older man of another he'd met on the road. White tufts of flyaway hair, like so much cotton, dancing a jig on the top of his head.

"Oh, an' 'bout the same," said the other man, leaning heavily on his shillelagh. "Ye know, an' I canno' complain."

"Then what in the devil will ye find to talk about?"

"I heard it's goin' to get cold as a witch's tit o'er the next few days." This from a short, roundish Irishman.

"An' I suppose the weatherman told ye it was goin' to snow as well?" A tall, gaunt gentleman, whose beaked nose and pointed chin struck a majestic profile beneath his checked cap, asked in reply.

"As a matter o' fact, he did," answered the stout man, with a vigorous nod of a head that, matching the torso, was snowman round.

"An' while he was at it, did he predict that ye'd still be a bleedin' eejit this time tomorrow?

"I was absolutely wrecked, I was. Stone dead knackered. Positively banjaxed after that night at the bar."

"Afore he knew it, Old Aachen had agreed to buyin' the whole gansey-load," said one shopkeeper to another as I was admiring the wares in the shop's front window.

"Amen convinced him, did he?" Said the other.

"Aye, yeah, yeah."

"An' that surprises ye?"

"Aye, Aachen's a bleedin' Scotsman. Wit' a hold on his money tighter than a camel's arse in a sandstorm. And stubborn. Fuck, an' he's stubborn."

"True, true, an' I know," replied the second man. "The Scotch are a stubborn lot, but the Irish are all 'bout gettin' their own way. We're fuckin' brilliant convincers.'"

"I'm just sayin', dog spelled backwards is God. Cat spelled backwards it Tac. 'Nuff said."

"Aye, an' it's dead easy, it is."

"The painters made a right bags o' the trim work."

Meaning: A botched job.

"Well, ye dunna' have to eat the head off me just fer bein' a better soccer player then ye."

Meaning: To rebuke verbally.

"Jaysus, Sean, stop foosterin' about an' pull me pint. It's donkey's years I been waitin' fer it."

Meaning (Foosterin'): Fiddling about.

Meaning (Donkey's Years): An inordinately long time.

"Patrick wanted to know if I'd lend him a hundred. I told him I will in me arse!"

Meaning: No way.

"I'm tellin' ye, the woman wouldna' leave me alone even after I told her to bite the back o' me bollix."

I think this one needs no translation.

Words and Phrases Common to both Villages

Banjaxed (hung over)

Jaysus

Massive

Brilliant

Thanks a million

Are ye headin'? (Are you heading out? Or, Are you leaving?)

Rough as a bear's arse (hung over)

What's the story? (How've you been?)

How ye keepin'? (How are you?)

Well dun, you.

What's the bleedin' bollox been up to now? (What kind of trouble has he gotten himself into now?)

Aye, an' I'm grand.

He could charm the scales off a concert pianist, he could.

Irish descriptors of someone drunk on his ass

Rat-arsed

Bollixed

Circling over Shannon

Plastered

Fluthered

Gee-eyed

Langered

Paralytic

Ossified

Go on the Batter

(To have) a great lip for the stout

Off me face

Pissed or piss-up

CHAPTER 11

Two Villages:
A Differing Resonance

Personal Note from the Author

The village I'd visited the year before, in County Cork, had been a different kind of magic from that of Connemara. Stepping off the bus on that day in early January 2016 had felt like coming home, giving me the opportunity to celebrate the part of myself I knew best. This was the playful, childlike part, all about laughter and happy endings, where no one ever dies, and love lasts forever.

Gripped by a strange sort of melancholy, I felt as if, in leaving this Connemara village behind, I'd come to the close of a chapter of my life. My time here seemed to have lasted a span of years rather than weeks and deepened my acquaintance with a different part of myself, one I recognized, but with which I'd lost touch.

An intimate bond, one I hadn't fostered since the long-ago days of summertime childhood spent sitting in the woods beyond my house, where I'd waited for the animals to join me in quiet communion.

A bittersweet melody hung in the air around this second village, circling the church steeples, and winding along the cobblestone streets. It slunk into alleyways and disappeared into pubs. This introspective stillness was something I understood and remembered from my childhood. Like an old friend, not quite forgotten, it beckoned me home.

The child I was bears little outward resemblance to the adult I've become, or more accurately, the persona that gets the most air time these days. Back then, it was easy to peg me as an introvert. Somewhere around age 35, I became an introvert in disguise. Not a façade, mind you, just an outward expression of an extroverted part of myself I'd kept under wraps in the decades before.

Being the youngest of four, with 15 years separating my sister and me and 12 between me and my twin brothers, my subjective experience, from the age of 6, was that of an only child. Every afternoon after school and for several hours a day during summer, I worked in my dad's drug store, dusting shelves and waiting on customers. I stood on an orange crate, so I could reach the antique crank cash register, ringing up Preparation H and cold medicine, birthday cards, mouthwash, and the insulin prescription for Old Floyd who lived out on State Road.

I was a serious child and related well to adults. Shy and awkward at school, I was often the target of ridicule and the kind of mean spirited teasing mastered in childhood and, for most of us, blessedly fades as we grow. When I was alone with my animals, losing myself in nature, or hanging out with my parents and my much older siblings, I felt whole, comfortable in my own skin, happy and secure.

But on the school bus, in the school cafeteria, on the playground, I was timid, silent, and, I'm pretty sure, strange. A broody kid, I hid deep within myself, daydreaming of being anyone but who I was.

The wild Connemara landscape and its people allowed me to explore this more introspective part of my inner being. It allowed me to integrate the seemingly disparate parts of my personality and emerge feeling more whole and more at peace with the various parts of myself.

Weeks passed like days and the month passed like a year. I owe this village in County Galway a debt of gratitude for bringing me into a more intimate relationship with myself.

EPILOGUE

Endings and Beginnings

Thank you all so very much for traveling with me. I hope you enjoyed the journey. Stay tuned for more Irish adventures from this grateful American.

Made in the USA
Middletown, DE
31 October 2019

77621614R00106